THE PHILANTHROPIST
with
TOTAL ECLIPSE *and* TREATS

Christopher Hampton was born in the Azores in 1946. As a child he lived in Aden and Egypt and at thirteen went to Lancing College. In 1964 he went up to New College, Oxford, to study German and French, and in 1968 he graduated with a First Class degree. He wrote his first play, *When Did You Last See My Mother?*, at the age of eighteen. It was first performed by Oxford undergraduates and subsequently put on at the Royal Court (June 1966). Since then, Christopher Hampton has worked on numerous original plays, adaptations and translations in the theatre, television and cinema.

THE PHILANTHROPIST
with
TOTAL ECLIPSE
and
TREATS

CHRISTOPHER HAMPTON

faber and faber

LONDON · BOSTON

This collection first published in 1991
by Faber and Faber Limited
3 Queen Square London WC1N 3AU

Printed in England by
Cox and Wyman Ltd Reading Berkshire
All rights reserved

A CIP record for this book is available from the British Library

ISBN 0-571-16218-5

For Bill Gaskill

CONTENTS

INTRODUCTION

The first of the plays here collected, chronologically speaking, is
Total Eclipse, which was written in 1967 and which I now tend to
think of, quite inaccurately, as the start of my career. This may
be because my earlier writings, as schoolboy or student, were
tentative experiments produced with the fluency and
unselfconsciousness of an amateur, whereas this was a
commissioned play more than likely to be professionally
produced in front of paying customers; or because I had always
considered my first play, *When Did You Last See My Mother?*,
given a Sunday-night production by the Royal Court Theatre
and kindly (no doubt too kindly) received by the critics, to be a
kind of dry-run for this much more ambitious piece; or even
because the beginnings of a literary career and the potentialities
of a writer's life were in a sense the very subject I was examining
in the play.

Language students at Oxford are given the option of
extending their course for a year in order to work abroad and
thus improve one or other of their languages. The amount of
time I had spent in my second year mounting my plays, first in
Oxford and then in London, combined with a no more than
vestigial ability to speak German, made this in my case a
necessity. My sympathetic and resourceful tutors found me a
post in one of those vast municipal theatres which, then as now,
possessed the resources to spend more money making armour
for a single production than a comparable English theatre might
receive in a year. So it was in Hamburg that I began writing the
play, on 1 April to be precise, which seemed an appropriate date
for so foolishly ambitious an undertaking.

My days in Hamburg were numbered. I had not enjoyed my
time in the city: but, more to the point, there had been a

misunderstanding about the nature of my *Studienstelle*, which turned out to be an honorary rather than a salaried position. I used this difficulty as an excuse to make an early getaway to Paris: where, under far more congenial circumstances, supporting myself with a translation job I was lucky to find, I pressed on into the summer with the play, which I eventually completed back in England in September.

Second plays were somewhat easier to place in those days than in the present, colder climate; still, production was by no means a foregone conclusion. The play had been commissioned by Michael Codron for the West End, but he soon decided, I'm sure correctly, that its dubious commercial prospects could never justify its expensive requirements, in terms of size of cast and number of locations. The Royal Court's initial response, meanwhile, was cautious. I began to be tormented by the idea that the piece, which had been at the forefront of my mind now for a number of years, would never be performed. Then, one day, unexpectedly, Robert Kidd (who had directed my first play) and William Gaskill (Artistic Director at the Royal Court) arrived in Oxford and asked me to read the play to them. They settled into the only two chairs in the room: I sat up on the bed and read. At the end there was a long silence, before Bill said, 'All right, we'll do it.'

This was not his only act of generosity towards me, as I'm happy to be able to acknowledge here. He also invented a job for me, which was given the resonant title of Resident Dramatist in the (successful) hope of attracting support from the Arts Council. And so, two weeks after graduating, I arrived for the start of rehearsals on *Total Eclipse* and a formative two years' work at the Royal Court.

The play was tepidly received at the time, but has since had more productions, I would guess, than any of my others; it seems to speak to a limited audience, but to speak to them loud and clear. Enthusiastic strangers have told me how much the play means to them in Utah and in Tokyo. For me, it was a means of posing a number of questions around a central puzzle, namely, what does it mean to be a writer? What could one reasonably hope to achieve? What were the pleasures and torments and what, if any, the responsibilities? Might one change the world, or would it prove beyond one's abilities even to change oneself? I still, of course, have no settled answers to these questions; but at that time it seemed that by examining two writers, Rimbaud and Verlaine, who had reached diametrically opposite conclusions on all these issues, despite their strong influence on one another, despite even the fact that they were lovers, some kind of fruitful internal debate might be triggered. For reasons I couldn't have explained then and still can't now, it seemed important to include the barest minimum of literary discussion in the play; to contemplate, in other words, only their lives and to leave with a scene which emphasized, despite the violence of their opposition, their fundamental solidarity as writers. Except in that final scene, I stuck firmly to the known facts ('Did you plunder my book?' Enid Starkie asked me when we met to discuss the play and seemed delighted when I admitted that I had), in the belief that reality will always yield more in the way of unexpected twists and poetic illumination than the most extravagant fictions.

Because the play is so central to me, I have had the greatest difficulty leaving it alone: consequently, there are four different published versions, two British and two American, of which I have chosen, for publication here, the third version, published after the revival at the Lyric, Hammersmith, in 1981, directed by David Hare. The fairly extensive changes for this production were made with David's help and encouragement and I haven't yet repented of them: but I still can't guarantee that this will remain my final version of *Total Eclipse*.

Molière was one of my special subjects at Oxford; and as I worked on *Le Misanthrope*, it occurred to me that in the climate of abrasive candour which characterized the late 1960s, Alceste would have been quite at home: whereas his opposite, a man concerned above all to cause no offence and be an unfailing source of sweetness and light, would very likely succeed only in raising hackles wherever he went. This notion was the germ from which *The Philanthropist* grew. As a setting which might be a modern equivalent of Molière's world, in which clever and envious people with a startling amount of leisure time sit around demolishing their colleagues, thoroughly insulated against any external pressures or upheavals, the university naturally suggested itself. Nowadays, no doubt, the bubble has burst and universities are as subject as the rest of us to the harsh rigours of market forces; but in 1968, as campuses erupted all over Europe, Oxford seemed as sleepy as ever, cocooned and self-regarding.

These are the factors which anchor *The Philanthropist* to its time; but I was also interested in applying Molière's method (comedy in which a character is examined in the light of a defining trait, such as hypocrisy or lust or avarice) to the study of what might technically be described as a virtue rather than a vice: compulsive amiability.

I began writing the play in February 1969, but pressure of work at the Royal Court, where I was now running the literary department, slowed me down and it was not until August, by which time I had agreed to stay on another year and acquired an assistant (and successor) in the shape of David Hare, that I was able to deliver. As with *Total Eclipse*, it was almost a year before the play reached the stage. During this time, I was happily employed providing new versions of *Uncle Vanya* (for Anthony Page at the Court) and *Hedda Gabler* (for Peter Gill at Stratford, Ontario), but *The Philanthropist*'s lack of progress was a constant source of anxiety. It was too soon for the Court to have refined what later became one of its deadlier techniques, refusal to produce the Resident Dramatist's play, but *The Philanthropist* was being passed from one distinguished director to another, without ever arriving at one whose dates or casting requirements or overall reservations about the play would allow him to sign the necessary bit of paper. Robert Kidd, meanwhile, fired from the Court, so he very plausibly claimed, for having received better reviews than he deserved, was in Manchester, working off a nine-month contract with Granada TV.

Eventually Robert was free, an exceptionally strong cast was quickly assembled and despite a quite serious outbreak of last-minute management jitters about the viability of the play, it opened on an early August evening in 1970, so sweltering that some unfortunate patron noisily passed out near the beginning of the second act: which made it particularly satisfying that the play's success (Michael Codron moved it to the West End, where it became, as far as I know, the Court's longest-running straight play) largely contributed towards the installation of the theatre's air-conditioning system. The week after the opening my time at the Court was up and I was on my own.

The text used here is the second edition, published to coincide with a revival of the play in Chichester in 1985. Apart from a certain streamlining, amounting to perhaps five minutes of cuts, it remains identical to the first edition, not to say the first draft of the play.

Treats was the last of the five plays I wrote for the Royal Court. It was also the shortest, the one which took longest to write and, by a considerable margin, the one which was least well received by the critics. It had its origins in two disparate ideas, one visual and one literary. First, I was haunted by the simple notion of a set which would represent a half-furnished room; and second, while I had naturally been delighted by the success of a translation I had made of *A Doll's House*, which had opened in New York in 1971 and caught the crest of the Women's Liberation wave, in retrospect there seemed something disturbing about this fashionable endorsement. Ibsen, after all, had designed the play to provoke; now it seemed the last word in social orthodoxy. And yet, as everybody knew, there were still just as many women trapped in unsatisfactory, restrictive and degrading relationships as ever there could have been in the 1870s.

Inclining my head to tradition, I began writing the play on 1 April 1974. It tormented me for almost a year, during which, at various times, I rented rooms in Oxford and London in order to try to knock it on the head. Finally, early in 1976, it reached the stage.

An author who sets out to provoke can hardly complain if his aim is achieved. And, in any case, slightly to our amazement, the play broke a box-office record at the Royal Court and went on, again with Michael Codron's help, to a respectable run in the

West End. Strangely enough, I found the critical reception rather bracing. All the same, the play formed a full-stop to the first phase of my career. I kept in touch with the theatre by writing translations, but I wanted to explore other avenues and it was more than five years before I attempted another original play. And then it was not for the Royal Court: I had a conviction it was a theatre for new writers, a description to which I could no longer lay claim. Still, it should be clear from the above that the plays in this volume were largely influenced by things I learned and supported by friends I made at the Court.

The version of *Treats* published here is the original text. Whether or not the memory of the agonies and mathematical rigours of its construction has caused me to shy away from the effort of revision, I can't say. In any event, the revival of the play at the Hampstead Theatre in 1989 made no changes. The critical response was noticeably mellower, but I was pleased to see the piece had not entirely lost its capacity to irritate.

Christopher Hampton, January 1991

THE PHILANTHROPIST

A Bourgeois Comedy

For Laura

C'est que jamais, morbleu! les hommes n'ont raison

Molière, *Le Misanthrope*

The first performance of *The Philanthropist* was given at the Royal Court Theatre, London, on 3 August 1970. The cast was as follows:

PHILIP	Alec McCowen
DONALD	Dinsdale Landen
JOHN	David Ashton
CELIA	Jane Asher
BRAHAM	Charles Gray
ELIZABETH	Tamara Ustinov
ARAMINTA	Penelope Wilton

Directed by Robert Kidd
Designed by John Gunter

The play is set in the near future and its characters are aged between 23 and 35.

CHARACTERS

PHILIP

DONALD

JOHN

CELIA

BRAHAM

ELIZABETH

ARAMINTA

SCENE ONE

PHILIP's *room. The room of a bachelor don, comfortable but not well-furnished, ordered but not tidy.* PHILIP *and* DONALD *sit, relaxed but attentive, one in an armchair, one on the sofa perhaps.* JOHN, *a younger man, is sitting in a wooden chair, a pile of papers on his knee. He holds a revolver.*

JOHN: You needn't think I'm not serious. Because I am. I assure you I am. Can't you see that? I've come here this evening because I think both of you are responsible for this and I think you deserve it as much as I do. If you hate me for doing it, that's your problem. It won't concern me. I just want you to have one vivid image of me, that's all, one memory to last all your life and never vanish, to remind you that if you won, I lost, and that nobody can win without somebody losing. Good-bye. (*He puts the revolver to his head.*) Bang. (*He smiles uneasily at them.*) Curtain. (*Silence.*)

Do you like it?

PHILIP: Very good. Would you like another drink?

JOHN: Oh, yes, thanks, er . . . Philip.

(PHILIP *pours a drink.*)

PHILIP: Ice?

JOHN: Please.

(*Exit* PHILIP.)

JOHN: He doesn't like it, does he?

DON: Oh, I don't know.

JOHN: He doesn't. I can tell.

DON: I'm sure he does like it.

JOHN: Do you?

(PHILIP *returns with the ice.*)

7

DON: Well. Yes and no. I mean there are some enormously
promising things in the play. Obviously it's basically a
conversation piece, but you do try to give the customers a
bit of everything – a touch of melodrama, the odd *coup de
théâtre*, humour, tragedy, monologues and pastoral
interludes, yes, yes, I like that, generous. But on the other
hand I think there are certain . . . lapses, which, you know,
detract from the play as a satisfying whole.

JOHN: You mean it's stylistically heterogeneous?

PHILIP: I think Don prefers to see it as an unsatisfying whole.
(*He laughs merrily and alone.*) Sorry. Would you like a
chocolate?

JOHN: No, thanks.

PHILIP: Don? I think I'll have one.
(*He helps himself to one, as he is to throughout this scene.*)

JOHN: Tell me what you don't like about it.

DON: Well, one thing is that character who appears every so
often with a ladder. The window cleaner. What's his name?

JOHN: Man.

DON: Yes. Well, I take it he has some kind of allegorical
significance outside the framework of the play. I mean I
don't know if this is right, but I rather took him to signify
England.

JOHN: No, no, erm, in point of fact he signifies man.

DON: Ah.

JOHN: Yes.

DON: Hence the name.

JOHN: Yes.

DON: I see.

JOHN: Although now you come to mention it, I suppose he
could be taken to represent England.

PHILIP: Is that two ns?

JOHN: What?

PHILIP: In Man.

JOHN: No, one.

PHILIP: Ah, well, you see, I thought it was two ns. As in
Thomas.

JOHN: Thomas?

8

PHILIP: Thomas Mann.

JOHN: Oh.

PHILIP: So I thought he was just meant to represent a window cleaner.

JOHN: Well . . .

PHILIP: Under the circumstances, I think you've integrated him into the plot very well.

JOHN: Thank you. (*He seems displeased.*)

DON: I always think the beginning and the end are the most difficult parts of a play to handle, and I'm not sure you've been entirely successful with either.

JOHN: Aren't you?

DON: I can't really say I like that Pirandello-style beginning. It's been done so often, you know. I mean I'm not saying that your use of it isn't resourceful. It is. But the device itself is a bit rusty.

JOHN: Yes, perhaps you're right. I'm not really very happy about the beginning myself. (*To* PHILIP) What do you think?

PHILIP: I liked it.

JOHN: Why?

PHILIP: No special reason, I just liked it. You shouldn't take any notice of me, though, I'm not really qualified to comment.

JOHN: You do lecture in English, don't you?

PHILIP: Yes, but in philology, not literature.

JOHN: Philology? Don't you find that incredibly tedious?

PHILIP: No, it's exactly the right subject for me. I'm fascinated by words.

JOHN: Individual rather than consecutive.

PHILIP: Yes. My only advice to writers is: make the real shapes.

JOHN: Pardon?

PHILIP: It's an anagram of 'Shakespeare' and 'Hamlet'.

DON: He's obsessed by anagrams.

JOHN: (*Coldly*) Really. (*Pause.*) What's your objection to the end of the play?

DON: It just doesn't convince me. It seems artificial. Do you really think he'd commit suicide in front of them like that?

9

JOHN: Yes. Why not?

DON: It doesn't seem to tie in with his character as we've seen it in the rest of the play.

PHILIP: I don't know. I liked it.

JOHN: You don't have to say that, you know. I'd much prefer to have honest criticism than your, if you don't mind me saying so, rather negative remarks.

PHILIP: Please take no notice of what I say. I always like things. I get pleasure from the words that are used, whatever the subject is. I've enjoyed every book I've ever read for one reason or another. That's why I can't teach literature. I have no critical faculties. I think there's always something good to be found in the product of another man's mind. Even if the man is, by all objective standards, a complete fool. So you see I'd like a play however terrible it was.

JOHN: So you think my play is terrible.

PHILIP: I didn't say that, I . . .

JOHN: I'm not an idiot, you know, I can take a hint.

PHILIP: Please don't get angry.

JOHN: (*Furious*) I am not angry! I just don't think there's any point in our discussing it any more, that's all. It's different with Don, Don has some constructive criticisms to make, which will probably be very helpful.

PHILIP: But I like the play more than Don does, I think it's very good.

JOHN: There's no need to be hypocritical.

PHILIP: I . . .

JOHN: I have no illusions about this play, you know. . . .

PHILIP: I . . .

JOHN: But I do think it has a little more merit than you give it credit for.

PHILIP: I'm sorry.

JOHN: Never mind.

    (*Silence.*)

PHILIP: Would you like a chocolate?

JOHN: No.

    (*Silence.*)

JOHN: (*To* DON) Now, what were you saying?

DON: I was just wondering whether the suicide is altogether justified.

JOHN: Oh, I think so. Given the kind of man he is. I think it could be quite powerful. I think perhaps he might put the revolver in his mouth. Then, if the back wall of the set was whitewashed, they could use some quaint device to cover it with great gobs of brain and bright blood at the vital moment. And just the two of them sitting there gaping. That would be wonderful.

(To illustrate, JOHN *puts the revolver into his mouth and presses the trigger. Loud explosion. By some quaint device, gobs of brain and bright blood appear on the whitewashed wall.*

PHILIP *and* DON *sit gaping. Long silence.)*

DON: Jesus.

*(*JOHN *has slumped back into the chair.* PHILIP *rushes abruptly from the stage.* DON *gropes shakily for the telephone and begins to dial.)*

BLACKOUT

(The first movement of the 2nd Brandenburg Concerto.)

SCENE TWO

A few days later. PHILIP, *alone, laying the dinner-table for six. A knock at the door.* DON *enters.*

DON: Hello. Am I too early?

PHILIP: No.

DON: I wondered if there was anything I could do to help.

PHILIP: No, it's all under control. Help yourself to a drink.

(DON *pours himself a Scotch.*)

DON: For you?

PHILIP: No, thanks. Not just yet.

(DON *sits down.*)

DON: Where's Celia?

PHILIP: In the kitchen.

DON: Are you all right?

PHILIP: Yes. Why?

DON: I don't know, you seem a little morose.

PHILIP: I am a bit.

DON: Why? You're not still upset about John, are you?

PHILIP: Well . . .

DON: I can't think why. You hardly knew the man.

PHILIP: That doesn't make any difference.

DON: Well, it should do. He was my friend, not yours. And I
haven't been sitting around brooding about it for days.
You're too sensitive, Philip, really. I mean, the whole thing
was just a grotesque accident.

PHILIP: I've never seen anyone dead before. I've never seen
anyone die.

DON: I don't know, the whole evening was a complete disaster. I
mean, apart from that. I only suggested we had it here
because I knew I'd hate the play, and I wanted someone

12

around who'd say something nice to him. I don't know why he got so ratty with you.

PHILIP: Well, I was very tactless.

DON: Nonsense, he was absurd. A sad case in many ways. There's no doubt he was very intelligent, but he had no idea how to write. That play was no good at all.

PHILIP: I rather liked it.

DON: I know you did, but it was no good. The ideas were there, but not the technique, it was far too cerebral.

PHILIP: Under the circumstances, I think that's a uniquely unfortunate adjective.

DON: What? Oh, oh yes. (*He laughs.*) Anyway, I see you've managed to get him off the wall.

PHILIP: Don.

DON: Sorry.

(*Silence.*)

PHILIP: Celia wasn't very sympathetic either. The first thing she said when I rang her up and told her about it was: 'I'm not surprised, he's always been ludicrously absent-minded.'

DON: Did she?

PHILIP: Yes.

DON: Come to think of it, absent-minded's even more unfortunate than cerebral. (*He laughs, recovers, shakes his head.*) No, it was a terrible thing to happen, really. (*He tries to look solemn, but is suddenly overcome by helpless laughter.*) Sorry. (CELIA *enters.*)

CELIA: What's the joke?

DON: John.

(*She puts some mats on the table.*)

CELIA: It's all very well for you to laugh, you didn't have to clean him up. He was all over the place.

PHILIP: Please, love . . .

CELIA: Philip had to throw away his Picasso print, didn't you? (*She heads for the door.*)

PHILIP: Can I do anything in the kitchen?

CELIA: I've yet to see any evidence of it.

(CELIA *goes out.*)

DON: Who's coming this evening?

13

PHILIP: Liz.

DON: Good.

PHILIP: Erm . . . Araminta, do you know her?

DON: Oh, really, where did you pick her up?

PHILIP: I didn't pick her up. She's one of the few people I come into contact with who has any interest in my subject at all. She seems quite intelligent, so I asked her.

DON: I don't think it's your subject she's interested in.

PHILIP: Oh?

DON: Haven't you heard about her?

PHILIP: No.

DON: The quickest drawers in the faculty. Old Noakes was telling me the other day he literally had to beg her to leave him in peace.

PHILIP: Did he really?

DON: Yes. So I should keep your hand on your ha'penny if I were you. (*Pause.*) Who else?

PHILIP: Braham Head.

DON: The novelist?

PHILIP: Yes. He's up here for a couple of weeks. Celia met him at some party and wanted to ask him. Do you know him?

DON: Slightly.

PHILIP: What's he like?

DON: Incredible prick. He's one of those writers who've been forced to abandon the left wing for tax reasons.

PHILIP: I quite like one or two of his books.

DON: They're dreadful. Dreadful. The man hasn't a glimmer of talent. And he's so rude and loud.

PHILIP: Oh.

DON: He left his wife last year. He said to her: 'Darling, I hope you're not going to be bourgeois about this, but I'm going to leave you and the children for a few months.'

PHILIP: What happened?

DON: She divorced him. Best thing she could have done. Their whole relationship was soured by her failure even to attempt suicide, which he apparently regarded as unforgivable. He likes to think of himself as a Romantic.

PHILIP: Surely he's not that bad?

14

DON: Worse. Worse. (*He broods for a moment.*) What about the
    Prime Minister, then?

PHILIP: What about him?

DON: Haven't you heard?

PHILIP: No.

DON: He's been killed.

PHILIP: What?

DON: Assassinated.

PHILIP: Has he?

DON: They've had nothing else on the radio all day.

PHILIP: How terrible.

DON: Most of the Cabinet as well.

PHILIP: Killed as well?

DON: Yes.

PHILIP: How did it happen?

DON: Well, shortly after the debate began today, this rather
    comic figure came bowling into the courtyard of the House
    of Commons on a bicycle: an elderly and rather corpulent
    woman wearing one of those enormous tweed capes, you
    know, ankle-length. She parked her bicycle, dropped the
    front wheel into one of those slots they have, and puffed up
    to the gallery, where she sat for a bit, beaming amiably and
    sucking Glacier mints. Then, all of a sudden, she leapt to
    her feet, produced a sub-machine-gun out of nowhere, and
    mowed down the front bench.

PHILIP: My God.

DON: Yes.

PHILIP: But . . . who was she?

DON: A retired lieutenant-colonel.

PHILIP: Salvation Army?

DON: No, no, she was a man. He gave himself up afterwards.
    He's completely round the twist. He says he did it to save
    Britain from the menace of creeping socialism.

PHILIP: But it's a Tory government.

DON: Nevertheless, he feels, if you can believe it, that the party
    is slithering hopelessly to the left. Said he felt called to be
    his country's liberator. Apparently, he's been practising in
    his garden in Wolverhampton for months.

15

PHILIP: God.

DON: Nine of them he got, and several others wounded. He probably could have managed more, but he seemed to feel an adequate statement had been made, so he trotted down the stairs, gave himself up like an officer and a gentleman and sauntered off to the cells whistling the Dam Busters' March.

PHILIP: But . . . what's going to happen?

DON: Oh, I don't know, coalition government, another election, something like that. It's not going to make much difference, whatever happens.

PHILIP: Isn't it?

DON: Not to us, anyway.

PHILIP: But . . . it's appalling.

DON: Yes. (*Pause.*) Worse things have happened. (*Pause.*) I must say, I think it was rather boring of him to do it on November the 5th. I suppose in the Tory Party that's the kind of thing that passes for aesthetics.

(CELIA *enters.*)

CELIA: Did you put the lemons in the 'fridge? I can't see them anywhere.

PHILIP: Oh, God.

CELIA: Don't say you've forgotten them. Honestly, I ask you to get one thing . . .

PHILIP: I'm sorry. I'll go and get them now.

CELIA: Everything's shut. We shall just have to have it without lemon, that's all.

DON: I think I've got a couple of lemons.

CELIA: Have you?

DON: Yes, in my rooms, in the fruit bowl, I think.

CELIA: Can I nip over and get them?

DON: Yes, sure.

CELIA: Thanks.

(*She moves over to the door.*)

PHILIP: Celia.

CELIA: Yes.

PHILIP: Anything I can do to help?

CELIA: No.

(CELIA *goes out.* PHILIP *looks unhappy.*)

DON: When is it you're getting married?

PHILIP: I, er, not sure really. Probably sometime in the vacation.

DON: Are you looking forward to it?

PHILIP: Well, yes, I think so. Why?

DON: Just wondered.

(*Silence.*)

PHILIP: You don't really think it's a good idea, do you?

DON: I don't know, Philip.

PHILIP: I mean, you don't really like her, do you?

DON: It's not that I don't like her, that's not it at all. She's very amusing and intelligent and attractive – it's just I sometimes wonder whether she's your kind of person.

PHILIP: What do you mean? You mean I'm not amusing and intelligent and attractive.

DON: Of course not. But you're rather . . . serious, aren't you?

PHILIP: I suppose so.

DON: And Celia isn't. In fact, she's rather frivolous.

PHILIP: But I like that.

DON: Oh, I'm sure you do. Sure you do. But it may cause you some trouble.

PHILIP: She is very malicious sometimes. She does seem to hate a large number of people I find perfectly harmless. Intensely. At first, I didn't think she really hated them, but I'm not so sure now.

DON: Have you ever thought about Liz?

PHILIP: Liz?

DON: Ever thought about marrying her?

PHILIP: No. Why?

DON: She's very fond of you, you know.

PHILIP: Really?

DON: Yes. I was talking to her about you the other day and I could see she was very fond of you.

PHILIP: Why, what did she say?

DON: Well, I can't remember exactly, nothing specific, it was just the way she talked about you. I'm sure she'd marry you like a shot if you asked her.

17

PHILIP: Do you think so?

DON: I'm sure of it.

PHILIP: She hasn't said anything to me about it.

DON: Well, she has her pride.

(*Silence.* PHILIP *broods.*)

PHILIP: And you think I should marry her instead of Celia?

DON: I didn't say that. I wouldn't dream of saying that.

PHILIP: But you think it.

DON: I'm just saying it would be possible if you wanted to do it.

PHILIP: Well, I don't.

DON: I know you don't. I'm sorry I mentioned it.

PHILIP: That's all right.

DON: I have this theory which I think is rather attractive. I think we're only capable of loving people who are fundamentally incompatible with us.

PHILIP: That's horrible.

DON: But attractive.

PHILIP: It's not really a very helpful thing to say.

DON: Take no notice. You know very well that unless you're a scientist, it's much more important for a theory to be shapely, than for it to be true.

(CELIA *enters with the lemons, which she puts down on the table.*)

CELIA: Christ, I must have a drink. (*She pours herself a Scotch and sinks into a chair.*)

DON: Did you find the lemons?

CELIA: Yes. Thanks.

DON: Isn't she marvellous?

(PHILIP *eyes* DON *uneasily.*)

PHILIP: I think so.

CELIA: So do I. I can't bear cooking: and I cook. I can't bear working: and I work. (*She smiles.*) And I can't bear Philip: and I'm marrying him.

PHILIP: It's all part of one basic condition.

CELIA: What?

PHILIP: You can't bear being a woman: and you are.

(CELIA *bristles.*)

CELIA: What do you mean?

18

PHILIP: It was a joke.

CELIA: Not a very funny joke.

PHILIP: It was about as funny as yours.

CELIA: Mine?

PHILIP: Yes, when you said you couldn't bear me and you were marrying me.

CELIA: You think that was a joke?

PHILIP: I . . .

CELIA: (*Laughing*) Your trouble is you have no sense of humour.

(PHILIP *is bested.*)

PHILIP: Sorry.

(*A knock at the door and* BRAHAM *enters. He is a tall, good-looking man, fashionably and expensively dressed. He carries a large paper bag.*)

BRAHAM: I hope I've come to the right place. (*He sees* CELIA.) Ah, hello love. (*He turns to* DON.) You must be Philip.

PHILIP: No, I'm Philip.

DON: I'm Don.

BRAHAM: Oh, yes, we've met, haven't we? Well, I'm Braham. Very nice of you to invite me.

PHILIP: It's kind of you to come.

BRAHAM: (*Turning to* CELIA) I went down to the market to buy you some flowers, my love, but they didn't seem to have any. So I got you this instead. (*With a flourish, he produces a cauliflower from the paper bag.*) As a token of my esteem.

CELIA: (*Dubiously*) Thanks.

BRAHAM: I'm sure you'll be able to find a niche for it.

(CELIA *takes it from him.*)

CELIA: I'll put it in the kitchen.

BRAHAM: Just the place.

(CELIA *goes out.*)

PHILIP: Can I get you a drink?

BRAHAM: Lovely girl.

PHILIP: Sherry or Scotch?

BRAHAM: (*Abstractedly*) Yes, please. (*He looks over towards the kitchen, as* PHILIP *stands by the drinks table, helpless with indecision.*) Lovely. She tells me you're getting married.

PHILIP: Yes. Erm. . . ? (*His courage fails him.*)

BRAHAM: What?

PHILIP: Nothing.

(*He decides on Scotch and pours it shakily.* BRAHAM *sits down.*)

BRAHAM: Well well well.

(*Silence.* PHILIP *hands him the glass.*)

BRAHAM: I observe that you are left-handed and that your maternal granny stands, or rather stood, six foot three in her socks.

PHILIP: Er . . .

BRAHAM: How can I tell, I hear you cry. (PHILIP *exchanges a slightly desperate glance with* DON *as* BRAHAM *sips his drink.* PHILIP *smiles weakly.*) I can see it in your . . . Did I ask for Scotch?

PHILIP: Well . . .

BRAHAM: Funny, I thought I said sherry.

PHILIP: Let me . . .

BRAHAM: No, no, never mind, never mind. Think nothing of it.

(*Silence.* PHILIP *takes a cigarette box from the table and offers one to* BRAHAM.)

PHILIP: Do you smoke?

(BRAHAM *takes one.*)

BRAHAM: Thank you.

(PHILIP *hands one to* DON. *Then closes the box and lights their cigarettes as he speaks, nervously.*)

PHILIP: I gave up last summer. It was months before I could make up my mind, but I finally decided I was more nervous about dying of cancer than I would be if I gave up smoking.

BRAHAM: Well, naturally.

PHILIP: No, no, what I mean is that I decided that the degree of nervousness I suffer in everyday life under normal circumstances without smoking although it was alleviated by smoking together with the added nervousness caused by the threat of ultimate cancer came to a sum total of nervousness it seemed to me in the end after lengthy as I say consideration greater than the original nervousness which had in the first place prompted me to take up smoking. If you follow my meaning.

(CELIA *has re-entered during this speech.*)

BRAHAM: I'm not sure I do.

PHILIP: No, well, I'm not expressing myself very well. I just mean it was paradoxical that I took up smoking because I thought it would be good for my nerves and discovered that even though it was I was more nervous after I'd taken it up than before because of the . . .

CELIA: What are you burbling about?

PHILIP: I'm not, I'm not expressing myself very well. I don't know what's the matter with me.

BRAHAM: I should have a cigarette if I were you.

BLACKOUT
(*Aria: 'Be joyful in the Lord' from Handel's 'Jubilate'.*)

SCENE THREE

After dinner. PHILIP, DON, CELIA, LIZ *and* ARAMINTA *are relaxing, talking, drinking coffee, brandy, etc., and smoking.* ARA-MINTA, *a rather large girl with a dramatically low-cut dress, sits on the floor, drinking crème de menthe.* LIZ, *a quiet, reserved girl (she does not in fact speak during the course of the scene) is dressed more soberly and sits watching, smiling to herself from time to time.*

BRAHAM: Tell me, what is the official line on Christ's navel?

ARAMINTA: On what?

BRAHAM: Christ's navel. When I went down to London on the train the other day, I fell into conversation with this priest, a very sprightly old gent, who told me that one of his proudest achievements was a polemic he'd written some years before against the view, which he said was widely held, that Christ had had no navel.

CELIA: Why shouldn't he have had a navel?

BRAHAM: Oh, well, it's all to do with the mysterious circumstances of his birth.

CELIA: Oh, I see.

BRAHAM: Anyway, he was a marvellous old boy. Marvellous. He said he lamented the passing of the closed compartment, no-corridor train and I asked him why and he told me that years and years ago, before he'd taken up the cloth and was sowing the occasional wild oat, he'd managed to strike up an acquaintance with a boy, seduce him and suck him off, all in the course of a journey between Bognor Regis and Littlehampton.

DON: Really?

BRAHAM: Yes.

ARAMINTA: Wonderful.

22

PHILIP: Er, shall we have the ten o'clock news?

BRAHAM: Why?

PHILIP: Well, I was just wondering what's happened about the Prime Minister and the government, you know . . .

BRAHAM: Oh, no, I think that would be unnecessarily depressing.

PHILIP: I just thought . . .

BRAHAM: In the car on the way over I heard them say the Queen had sent for the Minister of Sport.

ARAMINTA: What for?

CELIA: Her trampoline needs re-stringing.

ARAMINTA: Who is the Minister of Sport, anyway?

DON: Edith somebody, isn't it?

ARAMINTA: Why's she been sent for?

BRAHAM: Well, presumably she's the senior uninjured Minister.

ARAMINTA: They're not going to make her Prime Minister, are they?

BRAHAM: No, they can't possibly. I don't know, though, it might be rather diverting if they did. I must say, the great thing about all this is it shows we're accepting our decadence with a certain stylishness.

DON: What do you mean?

BRAHAM: Well, I think most people would agree that this has become a fairly sophisticated country. But I've always thought of sophistication as rather a feeble substitute for decadence. I mean I'm not saying everyone should go round assassinating people, but you must admit the way this man went about it did show a kind of rudimentary dramatic flair.

DON: I'd say he was a lunatic.

BRAHAM: Oh, yes, very probably. But like a lot of lunatics he's got one or two very shrewd ideas rattling around in his head.

DON: Like what?

BRAHAM: Like accepting our decadence without trying to go on pretending we're morally superior to the rest of the world. Like realizing that socialism is about as much use to this country as . . . a pogo-stick to a paraplegic.

23

DON: That's an extraordinarily repulsive image.

BRAHAM: What? Oh, yes, I suppose it is, really. Sorry, it just sprang to mind.

ARAMINTA: I thought it was very expressive.

BRAHAM: Thank you, Araminta.

DON: Do you really think that? About socialism?

BRAHAM: My dear chap, what I think about socialism is neither here nor there. Listen, when I was younger, I was a passionate Lefty writing all kinds of turgid, earth-shaking stuff which was designed to set the world to rights and which no publisher would have touched with a pitchfork. But eventually I realized, and what a moment of five-star disillusionment that was, that it wasn't going to work. Governments would not tumble at the scratch of my quill. I was just one little person in this enormous bloody world. God, in his infinite wisdom, had given me the ability to create essentially frivolous entertainments, which were enjoyed by enough essentially frivolous people for me to be able to amble comfortably through life. Naturally, it distresses me that people are wasting their energies killing each other all over the world, and of course I'm sorry thousands of Indians starve to death every year, but I mean that's their problem, isn't it, if they will go in for all this injudicious fucking. I actually used to think that in some obscure way it was my fault.

DON: You've got over that now, have you?

BRAHAM: Well, I have, yes. Nowadays, if I get one of those things through my letter-box telling me I can feed an entire village for a week for the price of a prawn cocktail, I tear it up, throw it in my waste-paper basket, go out to my favourite restaurant and order a prawn cocktail.

DON: And do you find that amusing?

BRAHAM: Oh, come now, the next thing you're going to say is what if everybody was like me. Fortunately for the world and even more fortunately for me, not everybody is. Look, if I actually get a concrete chance to help people, then I do.

ARAMINTA: Yes, I saw that TV appeal you did a few weeks ago.

DON: What was that for?

BRAHAM: Twenty-five guineas.

DON: I meant, on behalf of whom.

BRAHAM: I know you did.

DON: Well?

BRAHAM: (*Playing up*) Oh, I don't know, it was an appeal on behalf of spavined children. Or something equally sordid.

DON: And did it raise much money?

BRAHAM: Enough to cover my fee.

DON: I'm sorry . . . I must say I find that rather disgusting.

BRAHAM: That's perfectly all right. Most people do. (*Pause. He turns sharply to* PHILIP.) Do you think I'm disgusting?

PHILIP: Er . . . no, I don't think so, no.

BRAHAM: (*To* ARAMINTA) Do you?

ARAMINTA: Oh, no.

BRAHAM: (*To* LIZ) You?

(LIZ *shakes her head.*)

BRAHAM: (*To* CELIA) What about you?

CELIA: (*Smiling*) No.

BRAHAM: (*Turning back to* DON) There you are, you see, that's quite a good average. Obviously, my living depends on disgusting a certain percentage of people. If I didn't disgust at least a substantial minority, I wouldn't be controversial, and if I wasn't controversial, I wouldn't be rich.

DON: That's the way it works, is it?

BRAHAM: More or less.

DON: And that's the purpose of it all, to be rich?

BRAHAM: I don't know whether it's the purpose or not, but it's the result. I used to feel terribly shifty about all the money I was making, but then I realized I belonged to that small class of people who make exactly what they deserve. I'm a product. If the public stop wanting me, I stop earning.

CELIA: But you're all right for the time being.

BRAHAM: Oh, yes.

ARAMINTA: What's the best thing about being a writer?

BRAHAM: Ah, well, the real bonus comes when one actually discovers one or two moral precepts lurking about at the back of one's head. Then one can base a book on them and enjoy the illusion that one has bought one's E-type with a

25

couple of really valuable insights, golden truths, you might say. (*He laughs heartily.*)

DON: Well, at least no one could accuse you of being self-righteous.

BRAHAM: No, but I think one would be forced to admit I was pretty complacent. What I mean is there's no point in feeling guilty about these things, there's only two alternatives, keep it or give it all away, and that's a very interesting proposition, as the rich man said to Christ, but don't call me, I'll call you.

CELIA: And egotistical too, I suppose that's necessary.

BRAHAM: Oh, absolutely. Self-obsession combined with the ability to hold opposite points of view with equal conviction. The marvellous thing is that if the internal logic is coherent, I know that even if I'm wrong, I'm right. Makes me what you might call an existentialist's nightmare.

DON: Or a hypocritical creep, some might have it.

BRAHAM: Yes. (*He shakes with laughter.*) Oh, God, I did upset some poor little journalist the other day. 'How would you describe your job?' she said, and I said, 'Well, I suppose you might describe it as a kind of subsidized masturbation.'

DON: Don't you really think any better of it than that?

BRAHAM: Certainly not. I hope you're not implying there's anything wrong with masturbation.

DON: Well, I, no, not exactly . . .

BRAHAM: I should hope not. Masturbation is the thinking man's television. Don't you agree?

DON: I can't say I really remember.

BRAHAM: You shock me. (*He turns to* PHILIP.) You're not like that, are you?

PHILIP: No. I mean, well, occasionally, sometimes, I do.

BRAHAM: I'm pleased to hear it. It's extremely good for you, you know. Ah, many's the time I've had to lay down the pen and slip off to the bog for a quick one. Always remembering the Dunkirk spirit. Never forgetting that Waterloo was won in the dormitories of Eton. Any more brandy, is there?

26

(PHILIP *pours* BRAHAM *a brandy, then sees to the other guests.*)

CELIA: (*To* DON) Wasn't that your pupil's problem?

DON: Who?

CELIA: The one who's just been sent down.

DON: Who, Boot? No, no, no, I don't think it was sexual fantasy that finished him off, it was the failure of his political fantasies.

BRAHAM: Ah, well, there you are, you see, that's what I mean.

DON: Very sad case, was Boot. James Boot. The more subtle of his colleagues used to call him Jack. His first year he was very quiet, very shy, and all his work was carefully done and scrupulously on time. Good, solid, second-class stuff. Then, the beginning of this term, he didn't turn up when we were fixing the schedules, and one of the others told me he was in bed. So I sent him a note telling him when to come for the first tutorial and what to do. But when the time arrived I got a note from him saying he couldn't come, he was in bed. I naturally assumed he was ill, so when I was next in college I thought I'd call in on him to see how he was. He's got one of those nasty new modern little rooms, and I knocked on the door and went in. It was about four o'clock in the afternoon, he was in bed, the curtains were drawn, the fire was on and the stench was incredible. We talked for a bit. He offered me a biscuit. Then, anxious to beat a hasty retreat, I said I hoped he would be better soon. Then he told me there was nothing wrong with him.

It seems he'd spent the long vacation studying various political and economic works which had plunged him into such a state of total despair, that he had decided to devise some kind of final solution. At the beginning of term he had laid in enormous supplies of soup, cornflakes, biscuits, coffee and sugar – and then gone to bed. Since then, he'd been in bed twenty-two hours a day, brooding, only getting up to fix himself a meal, and never leaving the room except for the odd trip to the lavatory. 'But, Boot,' I said, 'but, Boot, why this sudden interest in politics? It's not even your faculty. Can't you, don't you think it would really be better, to turn your attention back to Wordsworth?'

Wordsworth, he said, with some passion, had nothing to do with anything, and his work, like all art, was a lot of self-indulgent shit which had no relevance to our problems and was no help at all to man or beast. I must say, the way he put it, it sounded quite convincing. I said to him: 'Look, it's not necessary to upset yourself like this. No one's expecting you to come up with an answer to all the problems of Western democracy.' 'Yes, they are,' he said, 'I am.' Further discussion seemed pointless. So I left him.

CELIA: And what happened?

DON: Well, he stayed in bed for the next six weeks, sending polite notes whenever he was supposed to be turning up somewhere, and I did nothing about it, because, because I rather admired him. And finally he reached a decision. He arrived at a conclusion.

He got out of bed one afternoon, took all his books down from the shelves, and piled them up in the middle of the room. Then he added all his papers and notes, wrapped the whole bundle up in his gown and set fire to it. He also set fire to the curtains, and turned the gas on. Then he put his dressing-gown on and left the building. A couple of his friends saw him wandering about and asked him jovially what he was doing up at that time of day. He told them he'd just set fire to the college. They carried on their way with much merry laughter. A moment later his windows blew out.

BRAHAM: Was there much damage done?

DON: His room was gutted. A little later they came to take him away. He's been formally sent down, which I think was quite unnecessary. I understand that since he's been admitted, he's been quite unable to move.

CELIA: I think that's very sad.

BRAHAM: I'd say he has a promising career ahead of him.

ARAMINTA: What as?

BRAHAM: A literary critic.

DON: I should think that's highly unlikely.

BRAHAM: I don't know. He sounds ideal. Do you know, I was actually forced to write a letter to some wretch a few weeks ago. He said my novel was too clever by half. So I wrote and said judging by the prose style of your review, I am forced to conclude, sir, that on the contrary, you are too stupid by half. (*He laughs.*)

DON: I really don't see what that has to do with Boot.

BRAHAM: Now you come to mention it, I suppose there is no logical connection. I forgot we were subject to the austere disciplines of academic tradition. I hope you're not going to give me fifty lines. (*He makes a mock appeal to* CELIA.) Are they all like this?

CELIA: No, Don is in a class of his own. He's the only one of my tutors who hasn't made a pass at me.

BRAHAM: Really?

CELIA: Yes. I don't count Philip, of course. Anyway, he doesn't teach me.

PHILIP: You're not going to tell me Professor Burrows made a pass at you?

CELIA: Ah, no, well I've made an interesting discovery about Professor Burrows. Professor Burrows is actually dead.

PHILIP: What do you mean?

CELIA: Well, I happened to see him with his wife just before one of those lectures he's been giving for decades, and she had her hand up inside his gown. Strange, I thought, and it was only later that it dawned on me what she was doing: she was winding him up. After that everything became clear – his voice, his colouring, the fact that he never takes any notice of what anyone says in seminars. He's been dead for years. They've installed a tape-recorder between his ears, and Mrs B. stacks him away in the 'fridge every night. That's it. It explains everything, the syllabus, everything. He's a contemporary of Beowulf.

DON: Who does that leave?

PHILIP: Johnson.

DON: Oh, inevitably.

CELIA: (*To* BRAHAM) Johnson is the Young Lion. He's a six-before-breakfast man. He lectures on Keats with such vigour and verve that the sticky young girls in the front row believe he is Keats. He's your typical Establishment misfit.

29

DON: And was he stylish about it?

CELIA: Stylish? It was one of the clumsiest gropes I've undergone for a long time. At the beginning of the tutorial, he poured me a drink and came and sat next to me on the sofa, and I thought this is it, fasten your seat belts. But he was just terribly nervous, he sat there looking strained and burbling on about the Romantics for three-quarters of an hour, and then suddenly he grabbed my further shoulder and wrenched me round so abruptly I emptied my sherry all over his camel-hair trousers. That threw him for a second. But he obviously had the sentence all worked out and he told me he thought I was very beautiful, and would I have dinner with him. I said I thought he'd better go and change his trousers before the next tutorial or his pupils would think he'd been at the Swinburne again.

BRAHAM: How did he handle that?

CELIA: Badly. Poor man, he was desperately embarrassed. He's never stopped apologizing ever since. I quite like him now. Rather him than Noakes any day.

DON: Noakes? (*He is amused at the thought.*)

CELIA: (*To* BRAHAM) Noakes, I must tell you, is not one of the world's ten best. In fact, he looks as if he's escaped off the side of Notre Dame. His face is enormous. And he sweats profusely, which makes him a very . . . shiny man. Ice-hockey matches could be played on his forehead. He's also kind of Neanderthal, I mean his knuckles scrape along the pavement as he walks. I must say, though, his grope was a great deal more thorough than Johnson's. Fortunately, his palms are so slimy, he wasn't able to get a proper purchase, as they say. But it was very nasty. He is, in every sense, oleaginous.

ARAMINTA: I think he's rather sweet.

CELIA: *Chacun à son goût.*

ARAMINTA: What do you mean?

CELIA: (*Feigning innocence*) Nothing.

BRAHAM: He certainly sounds extraordinarily repulsive.

ARAMINTA: I think she's exaggerating.

BRAHAM: No, no, he sounds very familiar to me. (*To* PHILIP)

What do you think about all this?

PHILIP: What?

BRAHAM: All your colleagues leching after your fiancé.

PHILIP: Oh, well, I think it's quite understandable. I don't really mind.

BRAHAM: Don't you? I'm sure I would.

PHILIP: I don't know, you know . . .

BRAHAM: How come you don't teach her? Is there some fifteenth-century statute against seeing your betrothed in school hours?

PHILIP: No, the thing is, I teach philology which is sort of optional, and old texts and things like that, which she doesn't do because she's a graduate.

BRAHAM: Philology?

PHILIP: Yes.

BRAHAM: My God, I thought that went out years ago.

PHILIP: No.

BRAHAM: I seem to remember it as the only subject which cunningly combined the boredom of the science faculties with the uselessness of the arts faculties.

PHILIP: Well . . .

BRAHAM: The worst of both cultures.

PHILIP: Most people seem to think that way. But I . . . find it interesting.

BRAHAM: Why? How?

PHILIP: Words. Words as objects. The development of words. Abuse of words. Words illustrating civilization. I mean, I can't go into it now, but all this new work that's being done in structural linguistics, I find absolutely fascinating.

BRAHAM: Structural linguistics, what's that, a yet more complicated method of over-simplification?

PHILIP: You might say so.

BRAHAM: You say you can't go into it now. Does that mean you don't think I could grasp it?

PHILIP: I'm sure you could grasp it, I just don't think it would interest you very much.

BRAHAM: Yes, you may be right.

PHILIP: But it does make me notice things. For instance, you're supposed to be, I mean you are, a successful writer, you make your living out of stringing words together. So it's very interesting for me to try to see how your language is formed.

BRAHAM: And how is it formed?

PHILIP: Well, I noticed just now you said something was extraordinarily repulsive, and I thought that was very revealing because it was a phrase Don used a few minutes ago.

BRAHAM: What are you getting at?

PHILIP: Well, it shows your ability for picking out and retaining striking phrases, subconsciously of course, but . . .

BRAHAM: Actually, as a matter of fact . . .

PHILIP: (*Enthusiastically*) See, that's another thing, the word 'actually', you use it a great deal.

BRAHAM: Why shouldn't I?

PHILIP: No reason why you shouldn't, you just do.

BRAHAM: I think you're being subtly insulting.

PHILIP: No, not at all, I . . .

BRAHAM: Yes, you are, go on, why don't you admit it?

PHILIP: I'm not.

BRAHAM: I think there's nothing cruder than an excess of subtlety.

PHILIP: No, look, I'm only making an observation. Like what you just said. That's something else. Your use of paradox. You've got it down to a fine art, it's a reflex action. You've digested that it's an extremely simple and extremely effective technique.

BRAHAM: You are being insulting!

(*Silence.* BRAHAM *is angry,* PHILIP *somewhat upset. The others are becoming embarrassed.*)

PHILIP: No.

(*Silence.*)

CELIA: He's not. He's just obsessed with the way people talk, that's all. Sometimes I think he's more interested in that than in what they actually say.

BRAHAM: What they what?

CELIA: Actually say.

32

BRAHAM: (*Triumphantly, to* PHILIP) See, I'm not the only one.

PHILIP: No, I know. Celia uses it quite often as well.

BRAHAM: (*To* CELIA) You're obviously my kind of person.

DON: Actually . . . (*He stops dead.*) Er, no, I mean, shit, yes, why not, actually . . . God, fuckit, I've forgotten what I was going to say now. (*Pause.*) Oh, yes, I was going to say Philip is quite remarkable with words. He can give you an anagram of any word or phrase, if there is one, in about two minutes, working it out in his head.

BRAHAM: Really?

DON: Yes.

CELIA: Try him.

PHILIP: No, I don't think . . .

BRAHAM: Ah, no, you're not going to get away with it as easy as that. I want an example of this. Give me an anagram of . . . give me an anagram of 'La Comédie Française'.
(*Silence.* PHILIP *concentrates.*)

PHILIP: In French?

BRAHAM: (*Magnanimously*) No, no, English will do. (*Pause. He returns his attention to the others.*) I always go there when I'm in Paris. God knows why. All that French classical theatre. Terrible camp old rubbish.

ARAMINTA: It's so stylized, isn't it?

BRAHAM: (*Ignoring her*) Mind you, the French never go there. Wouldn't go near it. It's full of Americans and Germans. Last time I went, I had this enormous American lady sitting next to me, and just as the lights went down, mark you, and they were banging that thing on the stage, she leant across and said, 'Excuse me, I haven't had time to read my programme, would you mind telling me what the play is about, because I just can't understand a word they're saying.' So I said, 'Well, madam, it's about a man who hates humanity so much that he would undoubtedly refuse to explain the plot of a world-famous play to an ignorant tourist.'

ARAMINTA: You didn't really?

BRAHAM: She thanked me. Profusely.

ARAMINTA: Which play was it?

BRAHAM: (*Coldly*) Three guesses. (*He broods for a moment.*) Anyway, I hate the Frogs.

PHILIP: A defence o' racialism.

BRAHAM: What?

PHILIP: A defence o' racialism. It doesn't quite work. There's an f missing. But it's the best I can do.

BRAHAM: (*Sourly*) Wonderful.

PHILIP: Thank you.

BRAHAM: Now perhaps you'll oblige us with a fart.

DON: It's exceptionally difficult to do, that. You should try it sometime.

BRAHAM: What?

DON: That anagram game.

BRAHAM: Oh, no, if we must play games, for God's sake let them be simple.

DON: Shall we play a game?

ARAMINTA: Oo, yes, let's. What about murder?

CELIA: (*Maliciously*) Postman's knock.

BRAHAM: I think it's a bit late for all that. I'm for a quick hand of Emptying the Brandy Bottle, and then I must be on my way.

PHILIP: (*Vaguely*) I've got some carpet bowls somewhere.

BRAHAM: (*Handing* PHILIP *his glass*) Some other time, perhaps. (*Silence.* PHILIP *pours brandy for* BRAHAM, CELIA *and* DON, *crème de menthe for* ARAMINTA. LIZ *covers her glass with her hand.*)

ARAMINTA: Are you writing a new novel?

BRAHAM: Yes, I am. It's nearly finished.

ARAMINTA: What's it about?

BRAHAM: It's about a social worker, who, after years of unremitting toil, finally sees the light, and renounces everything to become a merchant banker. I'm going to give it a really unfashionable happy ending. It's going to finish with his marriage to a sensitive film star.

ARAMINTA: Sounds intriguing.

BRAHAM: If it does as well as the last one, I'm going to have to leave the country.

ARAMINTA: Why?

BRAHAM: Tax. The tax system is absolutely iniquitous. What do they do with it all, I don't know. You'd think they'd make some sort of reasonable allowance. After all, I am a dollar-earner.

ARAMINTA: But the system's always been weighted against artists, hasn't it?

BRAHAM: Yes, all that's in the book. Although it's mainly, as I say, about this self-sacrificing character who gives up the comforts of moral superiority for the harsh realities of high finance. Should bring foam to the lips of the progressives. It'll be one up the noses of all the self-appointed salt of the earth who preach the revolution in the happy and comfortable knowledge that it'll never come.

DON: There are some people who believe in it, you know.

BRAHAM: (*Acidly*) There are some people who believe in God. (*Silence.*)

DON: I don't really see what that has to do with it.

BRAHAM: No, well, never mind, perhaps you're right. (*He empties his glass.*) In any case, I must be getting along. It's been a delightful evening. (*He looks over to* CELIA.) Can I give anyone a lift? Only one of you, I'm afraid, because it's only a two-seater.

ARAMINTA: Yes, please.

BRAHAM: Er, right, OK, where do you live?

ARAMINTA: Just round the corner, actually.

BRAHAM: Oh, well, that's all right, if it's very nearby, you can squeeze in the back, and I can take someone else. (*To* CELIA) Where do you live?

CELIA: Bradley Road.

BRAHAM: Is that far?

CELIA: About half an hour's walk.

BRAHAM: OK, fine.

CELIA: I think perhaps I should stay and clear up a bit.

PHILIP: No, that's all right, love, I'll do it.

CELIA: (*Meaningfully*) But I'd like to stay.

PHILIP: No, it'll be quite all right, you've done enough work for this evening.

DON: Come to think of it, Araminta, it'd probably be easier if you come with me. I shall be driving Liz back.

PHILIP: I'm sorry I haven't got my car. I lent it to a friend this evening.

BRAHAM: Right, good, that's all settled then. (*He gets up, turns to* CELIA.) Shall we be off?

CELIA: (*To* PHILIP) Are you sure you don't want me to stay?

PHILIP: Quite sure.

CELIA: Right then.

(BRAHAM *and* CELIA *move over to the door.*)

BRAHAM: Thanks again. Lovely to meet you. And may all your troubles be lexicological ones.

PHILIP: I'll show you out.

BRAHAM: Good night.

ARAMINTA: Good night.

DON: (*Charming*) Good-bye.

(PHILIP *shows them out amid general salutations*.)

DON: Miserable bugger. (*Pause. He gets up.*) Are we all ready, then?

(LIZ *gets up,* ARAMINTA *remains seated.*)

ARAMINTA: Perhaps . . . it's a terrible mess. Perhaps I'll stay and give him a hand.

DON: It's a kind thought. I don't suppose he'd let you.

ARAMINTA: I don't know, I might be able to persuade him.

(PHILIP *re-enters.*)

PHILIP: You going as well?

DON: Yes, I think we'd better.

ARAMINTA: I'm going to stay and help you clear up.

PHILIP: Oh, no, that's all right.

ARAMINTA: Then you can walk me home. How's that for a bargain?

PHILIP: Well . . .

ARAMINTA: Fresh air will do you good.

PHILIP: Well, all right, that's very kind.

(DON *and* LIZ *are by the door.* PHILIP *goes over and shows them out. Sounds of leave-taking from the hall.* ARAMINTA *starts piling plates in a fairly desultory way.* PHILIP *returns.*)

PHILIP: It's very good of you, this.

ARAMINTA: Nonsense. You just sit down.

(PHILIP *sinks down on to the sofa, sighing.*)

PHILIP: Just stick them in the kitchen. My man will do them tomorrow.

ARAMINTA: Tired?

PHILIP: Exhausted.

ARAMINTA: It was a great success.

(PHILIP *smiles wanly. Silence.* ARAMINTA *pauses in her work.*)

ARAMINTA: What time does he come in?

PHILIP: Who?

ARAMINTA: Your man.

PHILIP: (*Uneasily*) About eleven, usually.

(*Silence.* ARAMINTA *leaves the table and moves round behind the sofa to look out of the window.* PHILIP *seems anxious. After some hesitation, he steals a glance at her.*)

PHILIP: Not raining, is it?

ARAMINTA: No.

PHILIP: Oh, good.

(ARAMINTA *wanders across until she is directly behind* PHILIP. *Then, she leans forward and begins to massage his temples gently. This has the effect of making him seem even less relaxed. After a time, she moves round and sits on his knee.*)

ARAMINTA: Hello.

PHILIP: Erm, hello.

(*She kisses him.*)

ARAMINTA: Is that nice?

PHILIP: Very. Could you, could you just move down a bit?

(*She does so, and* PHILIP'*s look of intense pain changes to one of acute anxiety.*)

ARAMINTA: Better?

PHILIP: Yes.

(*She kisses him again.*)

ARAMINTA: Shall we go to bed?

(*Brief silence.*)

PHILIP: I'll . . . just go and get my coat.

(ARAMINTA *stares at him for a moment in blank incomprehension, then realizes what he means. She stands up.*)

ARAMINTA: I meant together.

37

PHILIP: Oh, I wasn't quite sure.
(*Panic overcomes him. He looks at his watch, stares fixedly at it for a moment.*)
ARAMINTA: Well?
PHILIP: Well . . .
ARAMINTA: Don't be too enthusiastic.
PHILIP: It's just . . . it's just . . .
ARAMINTA: What?
PHILIP: (*Clutching at a straw*) I haven't any, haven't got any . . .
ARAMINTA: Not necessary.
PHILIP: Oh.
ARAMINTA: If you don't want to, just say so . . .
PHILIP: No, no, I do, I do.
ARAMINTA: . . . and I'll go home . . .
PHILIP: No.
ARAMINTA: . . . it's not a matter of life or death to me, you know.
(PHILIP *stands up.*)
PHILIP: I know, I'm sorry, it just took me a bit by surprise, that's all.
(*He kisses her.*)
ARAMINTA: Didn't look like a very pleasant surprise.
PHILIP: Please. (*He kisses her again.*) It's just that I'm shy, that's all.
ARAMINTA: I know. I love shy men.
PHILIP: All right now?
ARAMINTA: Yes.
(*They embrace.*)
ARAMINTA: Is that the bedroom, through there?
PHILIP: Yes.
(*She moves across to it, turns at the door.*)
ARAMINTA: Don't be long.
(PHILIP *smiles weakly at her, as she exits, then sinks down on to the sofa again. A moment later he gets up, moves over to the table, takes a cigarette from the cigarette box, and puts it in his mouth, where it hangs limply for a moment. Then he returns it to the box, and sighs deeply.*)
PHILIP: God help us all.

(He exits wearily and reluctantly into the bedroom, leaving the stage empty.)

CURTAIN

(Aria: 'O wie ängstlich' from Mozart's 'Die Entführung aus dem Serail', followed, during the interval, by the aria: 'Dies Bildnis ist bezaubernd schön' from 'Die Zauberflöte', and the aria: 'Wenn der Freude Tränen fliessen' from 'Die Entführung'.)

SCENE FOUR

The opening of Purcell's ode: 'Welcome, welcome, glorious morn'. The next morning. ARAMINTA *is sitting at the table with a cup of coffee and a cigarette, reading the newspaper. The music fades. There is a knock at the door. She looks up, startled.* CELIA *walks in, sees* ARAMINTA *and stops dead.* ARAMINTA *gets up, quickly. It takes her a moment to regain her composure.*

ARAMINTA: Er, hello.

CELIA: Good morning. Is Philip in, by any chance?

ARAMINTA: I believe he's in the bath.

CELIA: Oh, really? (*The shock is beginning to leave her.*) Alone?

ARAMINTA: I think so.

CELIA: You're slipping. (*She helps herself to a cigarette, lights it.*) Well, I must say, I am surprised.

ARAMINTA: Why?

CELIA: I never thought you'd manage to add Philip to your collection.

ARAMINTA: What do you mean?

CELIA: You know, I sometimes think, although I can never quite bring myself to accept it, that you really are as thick as you pretend to be.

ARAMINTA: You're very offensive this morning.

CELIA: I'm very offended. I don't know why you couldn't have left him alone. Do you write all their names up in a Book of Remembrance, or something? Do you give every hundredth one a pair of gold cuff-links with some discreetly erotic motif? Are you thinking of turning professional?
(*Silence.*)

ARAMINTA: Would you care for some coffee?

CELIA: No, I would not.

40

ARAMINTA: Don't be like that.

CELIA: Why not?

ARAMINTA: It wasn't serious.

CELIA: Why did you bother, then?

ARAMINTA: That's an absurd question. I just felt like it.

CELIA: Didn't you stop to consider the consequences?

ARAMINTA: There are no consequences. At least, there wouldn't have been, if you hadn't walked in just now. The idea was, you see, that you weren't going to find out about it.

CELIA: Well, all I can say is, there's no accounting for taste.

ARAMINTA: What, his taste or my taste?

CELIA: (*Flustered*) His taste.

ARAMINTA: You should know, you're engaged to him.

CELIA: That's my business.

ARAMINTA: I know. I hope he gives you better service than he gave me.

CELIA: What do you mean?

ARAMINTA: Never mind.

CELIA: How can you be so cheap and disgusting?

ARAMINTA: Practice makes perfect.

CELIA: Yes, apparently.

ARAMINTA: And where did you spend last night?
(*Silence.*)

CELIA: Look, will you, will you please tell Philip that I called . . .

ARAMINTA: Why don't you wait and tell him yourself?

CELIA: . . . and that I won't be calling again.

ARAMINTA: That's ridiculous, you can't mean that, I can't tell him that.

CELIA: (*Moving to the door*) Don't, then.

ARAMINTA: There's no need to be like that about it, honestly. I promise you I won't be coming back for more. If that's the word.

CELIA: Well, neither will I.
(CELIA *storms out.* ARAMINTA *sits down, reflects for a moment, then returns to the paper. A moment later,* PHILIP *enters. He and* ARAMINTA *greet each other warily. He pours a cup of coffee, sugars and stirs it, then moves over to the window.*)

PHILIP: It's a good view, isn't it?

ARAMINTA: Yes, very nice.

PHILIP: You can see the river. In the distance. When the tide's in. (*Longish pause.*) It's out at the moment. (*Pause.*) Look, I'm sorry about last night.

ARAMINTA: No need to be.

PHILIP: Yes, it was awful. I mean, it must have been awful for you.

ARAMINTA: No, it wasn't.

PHILIP: The thing is, I suppose I was a bit taken by surprise. It's the first time that's ever happened to me.

ARAMINTA: You're not . . . you're not trying to tell me you were a virgin?

PHILIP: No, no. No, not that.

ARAMINTA: Oh, you mean it's the first time you've not been able to make it?

PHILIP: Not that, either.

ARAMINTA: What then?

PHILIP: It's just the first time I've ever been asked like that, point-blank. I think I must have found it rather disconcerting.

ARAMINTA: And that's why you were rather . . . disconcerted.

PHILIP: Yes.

ARAMINTA: It doesn't matter at all. It happens more often than you might think. Especially the first time.

PHILIP: Oh, does it?

ARAMINTA: (*Breezily*) First-night nerves.

PHILIP: What a . . . colourful description.

ARAMINTA: Nothing to worry about. If at first you don't succeed . . .

(PHILIP *smiles, appalled.*)

PHILIP: Have you had some breakfast?

ARAMINTA: Coffee, I've had.

PHILIP: Would you like something to eat?

ARAMINTA: I don't think so, thanks.

PHILIP: I usually have an enormous breakfast.

(*Silence.*)

ARAMINTA: Don't worry.

42

PHILIP: What about?

ARAMINTA: Anything. I don't mind. At least you're kind and gentle. It's more than can be said for most of them.

PHILIP: What do you do it for?

ARAMINTA: Company. I like being with people. And if you're with them, you might as well do it as not. Don't you agree?

PHILIP: I don't . . . disagree.

ARAMINTA: They tell me I'm a classic case, because my uncle raped me when I was twelve. I've never quite been able to see the connection, you'd think it would have put me off, wouldn't you?

PHILIP: Yes.

ARAMINTA: I suppose it did rather take the romance out of things.

PHILIP: Haven't you ever . . . been in love with anyone?

ARAMINTA: Not really. I did have an affair with a gypsy when I was about fifteen. I used to climb out of the window every night and cycle about three miles to meet him. He never used to say very much. I was terrified of him. It went on for about a month, then he moved on, and I remember being very sad. But I don't know that I was in love with him. I quite often hero-worship people, that quite often happens, but it's difficult to go on with once you know them a little . . . better.

PHILIP: And are they often cruel to you?

ARAMINTA: Oh, yes, I'd say so, what I am seems to upset them in some kind of way. I always seem to bring out the worst in people. There was one who stole my clothes when I was asleep one night and locked me in the bedroom of his flat for about three weeks. He was the worst. He hardly gave me any food. He used to threaten me with a knife. Once he nearly strangled me.

PHILIP: What happened?

ARAMINTA: Well, in the end he came and let me out. I was nearly going mad. There seemed no logical reason why I shouldn't be there, in that disgusting room, for ever. But finally he let me go. It was strange. He was so abject. He kept apologizing all the time, asking me to forgive him.

Then, when I was leaving, he asked me to marry him.

PHILIP: God.

ARAMINTA: I felt so sorry for him.

PHILIP: Yes. (*Pause.*) It must have been terrible.

ARAMINTA: I could tell you things you would never forget.
   (*Silence.*)

PHILIP: Why . . . why do you do it all?

ARAMINTA: That's rather a silly question.

PHILIP: Yes, yes, it is, sorry.

ARAMINTA: I get lonely. I hate sleeping alone. All that.

PHILIP: Yes.
   (*He smiles at her. She gets up.*)

ARAMINTA: Well, I suppose I'd better get dressed.

PHILIP: Yes, I'll fix some breakfast. What would you like?
   (ARAMINTA *takes his hand.*)

ARAMINTA: Come on.

PHILIP: What?

ARAMINTA: We'll be all right this time.
   (PHILIP *hesitates. A moment of private dilemma.*)

PHILIP: No.

ARAMINTA: No?

PHILIP: Really.
   (ARAMINTA *lets go his hand.*)

ARAMINTA: Well, all right.

PHILIP: No, listen, I think I'd better explain.

ARAMINTA: There's no point in explaining, love, you either
   want to or you don't.

PHILIP: No, I mean about last night.

ARAMINTA: I've told you . . .

PHILIP: I know it was my fault, I was very weak-minded.

ARAMINTA: Weak-minded, was it?

PHILIP: I should never have agreed, I knew it would be a
   disaster.

ARAMINTA: Well, I could see you were thrown by the directness
   of my approach.

PHILIP: It wasn't that, it was just, I didn't really want to.

ARAMINTA: I know, it's funny how important fidelity is to some
   people. I mean, it's something that never occurs to me.

44

PHILIP: It wasn't that, the truth is, I don't really find you attractive.

(*Silence.*)

ARAMINTA: I see.

PHILIP: No, don't be upset, it's my fault, my taste has always been terribly limited.

ARAMINTA: (*Upset*) I'm not upset.

PHILIP: No . . .

ARAMINTA: I don't know why you should think that.

PHILIP: It's just . . .

ARAMINTA: I mean, I don't exactly find you irresistible.

PHILIP: No. I'm sorry about it all.

ARAMINTA: So you should be.

PHILIP: Yes.

ARAMINTA: It might have been easier if you'd said last night.

PHILIP: Yes.

ARAMINTA: Don't you think?

PHILIP: Yes.

ARAMINTA: I don't know, who do you think you are?

PHILIP: Well . . .

ARAMINTA: Anyway, I shan't offend your sight much longer.

PHILIP: You don't offend my sight . . .

ARAMINTA: I'll get dressed and leave you alone.

PHILIP: . . . that's not it at all.

ARAMINTA: Won't take me a minute.

PHILIP: Please.

ARAMINTA: A lot of people do find me attractive.

PHILIP: I'm sure. It's just me. I can't seem to like women unless they're . . .

ARAMINTA: There's no need to go into it.

PHILIP: No, all right.

ARAMINTA: Not that you did.

(*She moves off towards the bedroom.*)

PHILIP: Can I get you some breakfast?

ARAMINTA: Will you please stop parroting on about breakfast?

(ARAMINTA *exits.* PHILIP *stands disconsolately for a minute, then pours himself a huge bowl of cornflakes, adding sugar and milk. He is about to begin eating when* ARAMINTA *returns,*

45

having dressed with extraordinary speed.)

ARAMINTA: There is just one other thing.

PHILIP: Look, please don't go.

ARAMINTA: There is one other thing I should mention.

PHILIP: What?

ARAMINTA: When you were in the bath.

PHILIP: Yes.

ARAMINTA: Celia.

PHILIP: What?

ARAMINTA: Called.

PHILIP: God. Why didn't you tell me?

ARAMINTA: I just have.

PHILIP: What . . . what did she say?

ARAMINTA: She seemed a bit put out.

PHILIP: Put out?

ARAMINTA: Yes. She asked me to tell you she wouldn't be
calling again.

PHILIP: What?

ARAMINTA: That was it, I think.

PHILIP: Why?

ARAMINTA: Well, as far as I could gather, it's not to do with
your religious beliefs.

PHILIP: What?

ARAMINTA: Why do you think, you half-witted buffoon?

PHILIP: Because you were here. (ARAMINTA *does not answer.*)
Oh, God.

ARAMINTA: Passion.

PHILIP: I don't know what to do.

ARAMINTA: No, I'm sure you don't.

(*She moves over to the door.*)

PHILIP: Wait. What did she say?

ARAMINTA: Well, naturally we discussed the weather. Then, as
I remember, she became rather impolite. (PHILIP *groans.*
ARAMINTA *softens.*) Look, I'm sorry it happened. There
was nothing I could do about it. I think I'd better go now.
(*She does so.* PHILIP *stands for a moment, uncertain. Then he
picks up the 'phone, dials a five-figure number and waits. No
answer. He puts the 'phone down. He wanders back to the*

46

*table, sits down, picks up the bowl of cornflakes and starts
eating.*)
BLACKOUT
(*Chorus: 'Vollendet ist das grosse Werk' from Haydn's 'Die
Schöpfung'.*)

SCENE FIVE

PHILIP *is sitting at his desk, working, later that day. A knock at the door.* CELIA *walks in.* PHILIP *gets up quickly. They look at each other for a moment, distraught.*

PHILIP: Love.
CELIA: I just came back to tell you I wasn't coming back.
PHILIP: I've been trying to 'phone you all day.
CELIA: I've been out.
PHILIP: Working?
CELIA: No, of course not, what do you think I am?
PHILIP: I . . .
CELIA: I suppose you've been working.
PHILIP: Yes.
CELIA: Typical.
PHILIP: I thought it would take my mind off things.
CELIA: And did it?
PHILIP: No.
CELIA: Even more typical.
PHILIP: Why?
CELIA: Did you hear what I said?
PHILIP: What?
CELIA: When I came in.
PHILIP: Yes, but listen . . .
CELIA: If you say 'I can explain everything', I'll punch your
    bloody teeth in.
PHILIP: But I can.
CELIA: I suppose you were discussing morphology all night. Or
    checking her vowel sounds.
PHILIP: No.
CELIA: It's so insulting, Philip. I mean you deliberately got rid

48

of me.

PHILIP: What do you mean?

CELIA: Well, I did ask you to let me stay.

PHILIP: You didn't.

CELIA: Of course I did. I couldn't have made it much clearer if I'd started unbuttoning myself.

PHILIP: But I thought you just wanted to help with the washing-up.

CELIA: You amaze me. You really do.

PHILIP: Christ, I wish you had stayed.

CELIA: Why?

PHILIP: I didn't realize you wanted to stay the night. Oh, God, I wish you had.

(*Silence.*)

CELIA: You're being cunning.

PHILIP: I'm not.

CELIA: Don't. It's most unlike you.

PHILIP: I'm not.

CELIA: Look.

PHILIP: What?

CELIA: Why did you ask her to stay?

PHILIP: I didn't. It's just she offered to help with the washing-up.

CELIA: If you didn't let me stay because you thought I wanted to do the washing-up, why did you let her stay when you thought she wanted to do the washing-up?

PHILIP: She insisted.

CELIA: And more to the point, why did you let her stay when you realized she didn't want to do the washing-up?

PHILIP: She insisted.

CELIA: And you gave in.

PHILIP: Yes.

CELIA: Well, why?

PHILIP: Because I didn't want to hurt her feelings.

CELIA: What about my feelings?

PHILIP: You weren't there.

CELIA: If you go on saying things like that to me, do you really expect I'm going to marry you?

49

PHILIP: I hope so.

CELIA: You're so incredibly . . . bland. You just sit there like a pudding, wobbling gently.

PHILIP: Do I?

CELIA: You're about as emotional as a pin-cushion.

PHILIP: I don't think that's true.

CELIA: Don't you?

PHILIP: No, I don't think so.

CELIA: Only you would sit there pondering the pros and cons of a fairly conventional simile.

PHILIP: It's more of a hyperbole really, isn't it?

CELIA: It's more of a fucking insult, that's what it really is, I think you'll find. Seeking a response, not a bloody inquest.

PHILIP: Oh, well . . .

CELIA: Inviting a retort, not a sodding debate.

PHILIP: I . . .

CELIA: You're talking about last night as if it were a conference on the future of the phoneme.

PHILIP: Am I?

CELIA: You're not even sorry!

PHILIP: Of course I am. Of course I am.

(*By now,* CELIA *is angry and upset.*)

CELIA: I'm going.

PHILIP: No, don't.

CELIA: I've said what I came to say.

PHILIP: Don't go before I tell you what happened.

CELIA: I know what happened, I don't want to hear the squalid details. I don't want to listen to your pathetic attempts at self-justification.

PHILIP: I'm not trying to justify myself. I just want to explain to you exactly what happened. Then you can make your mind up.

CELIA: All right, go on, tell me. (*Pause.*) Try to make it as entertaining as possible.

PHILIP: Well . . . well . . . she asked me to go to bed with her, just like that. It took me so much by surprise, I could think of no delicate way to refuse. So I accepted. The whole thing was a complete fiasco. No good at all. Then, this morning she suggested we try again, and I had to tell her it was no use, because I quite honestly didn't find her attractive.

CELIA: Not many laughs in that.

PHILIP: No. No, I suppose there weren't.

CELIA: What happened next?

PHILIP: She left.

CELIA: Immediately?

PHILIP: Yes. She seemed very angry.

CELIA: Fancy that.

PHILIP: I handled it badly.

CELIA: You might say so. Sounds to me like a triumph of emotional incompetence.

PHILIP: Well, that's how it happened.

CELIA: And I suppose you think that makes it all right, do you?

PHILIP: What do you mean?

CELIA: I suppose you think because you were bullied into doing something you then failed to do anyway, it's as if the whole thing didn't happen.

PHILIP: No.

CELIA: Did it never occur to you that I might prefer it if you brazened the whole thing out and said, yes, it was all planned, it was your final fling before we got married, or something like that?

PHILIP: But it wasn't.

CELIA: You're so damn literal-minded. I mean you might have just said you'd done it and you were sorry and it wouldn't happen again – instead of saying all right, not to worry, I was an abject failure, so that doesn't count.

PHILIP: I didn't say that.

CELIA: No, you didn't even say that.

PHILIP: All I can do is tell you what happened and leave it up to you.

CELIA: Well, if you leave it up to me, I shall have to say I can't possibly undertake to spend my life with someone so hopelessly weak and indecisive, he's going to leave every major issue up to me.

PHILIP: That's not very fair.

CELIA: We're not playing croquet, you know.

51

PHILIP: No, but in this case I've made my half of the decision. I want to marry you. So it's only up to you in the sense that you haven't decided yet.

CELIA: Oh, you do make me so angry.

PHILIP: Why?

CELIA: You never understand what I'm trying to say.

PHILIP: Maybe not, but I think I usually understand what you do say.

CELIA: God, you're completely impossible.

PHILIP: (*Bewildered*) I'm sorry. (*Pause.*) I suppose I am indecisive. (*Pause.*) My trouble is, I'm a man of no convictions. (*Longish pause.*) At least, I think I am. (CELIA *starts laughing.*) What's the joke?

CELIA: I am fond of you.

PHILIP: (*Lost*) Are you?
(*Silence.*)

CELIA: I'm afraid my plan didn't work at all.

PHILIP: Plan?

CELIA: I was going to use it as an excuse. I mean it seemed like a perfectly good excuse.

PHILIP: Use what as an excuse? What for?

CELIA: For . . . finishing.

PHILIP: I don't understand.

CELIA: Well, I've been thinking, you see, really, for a long time, that we aren't really compatible.

PHILIP: Oh.

CELIA: I always used to think you were just the sort of person I'd been looking for. Someone fairly intelligent and reliable and kind and safe and a little bit dull. Somebody who admired me and thought what I said was worth listening to, not just worth tolerating.

PHILIP: But you were wrong.

CELIA: Yes, I think perhaps I was wrong.

PHILIP: I see.

CELIA: And after what happened last night, I thought I'd better come over to discuss things with you. And when I found Araminta here, I thought that gives me an excuse not to discuss things with you, I can just leave you, and make you think it's your fault.

PHILIP: (*Confused*) How do you mean, what happened last night? You didn't know about it, did you?

CELIA: I mean what happened to me.

PHILIP: Oh. What did happen to you?

CELIA: Braham took me back to his hotel.

PHILIP: Oh.

CELIA: And I stayed the night there.

PHILIP: But . . . why?

CELIA: I don't know, he went on at me. And I finally thought oh well, why not, I was still very angry about your not letting me stay. I don't know why. I felt dreadful this morning. He kept saying that creative artists had a much more consuming sexual urge than ordinary people. He told me that's why Bach had thirty children.

PHILIP: And were you convinced by this argument?

CELIA: No.

PHILIP: But you still. . . ?

CELIA: Yes.

PHILIP: Why? I don't see why.

CELIA: Well, he's so confident and self-assured, I don't know why. I just suddenly felt like it, don't go on about it.

PHILIP: And is that what you want?

CELIA: I don't know, I suppose so. Not him, I don't mean him, he's awful, but something like that.

PHILIP: What makes you think he's awful?

CELIA: Well, it was this morning, the way he behaved this morning, that really turned me off him. For one thing, he was so nasty about you.

PHILIP: Was he?

CELIA: Yes, he really hates you. All the time yesterday evening, he thought you were taking the piss in a particularly subtle way.

PHILIP: Really?

CELIA: And then when I'd argued with him a bit and told him that wasn't in your nature, he finally agreed and said, yes, come to think of it, he supposed you were far too boring to do anything as enterprising as that.

53

PHILIP: Well, he's right there, isn't he?

CELIA: What do you mean?

PHILIP: Isn't that what you think?

CELIA: Of course not, don't be so rude.

PHILIP: I'm sorry, I thought that's what you just said.

CELIA: I think you get a perverse kick out of running yourself down.

PHILIP: No, I don't. I don't think I do.

CELIA: Anyway, I defended you, even though I knew you wouldn't have defended yourself.

PHILIP: Why did he hate me, I don't know, I didn't hate him.

CELIA: Didn't you?

PHILIP: No, I thought he was quite amusing.

CELIA: And do you hate him now?

PHILIP: No.

CELIA: Not even after everything I've told you?

PHILIP: I don't suppose he's very happy.

CELIA: (*Angrily*) And are you happy?

PHILIP: No.

CELIA: Well then.

PHILIP: Not at the moment.

CELIA: (*Offended*) Oh, I see.

PHILIP: I mean . . . I mean, I hope to be. I have been. I hope I will be. (*He moves over to the window.*) Look. The tide's in. It's a lovely day, look. (*Pause.*) It's very rare to have a day as fine as this in November.

CELIA: Yes.

PHILIP: (*Smiling*) Just when one was getting used to the idea of winter. (*Pause.*) I'm glad you defended me. I don't see what he has against me.

CELIA: That was only the beginning. He got far worse.

PHILIP: In what way?

CELIA: It was when he read about R. J. Morris in the paper.

PHILIP: What about him?

CELIA: Haven't you looked at the paper today?

PHILIP: No, I couldn't, it was all full of stuff about the Prime Minister, I thought it would be too upsetting.

CELIA: Well, R. J. Morris was murdered yesterday as well.

PHILIP: He wasn't!

CELIA: Yes, apparently there's some gang of lunatics about, whose intention is to knock off twenty-five of the most eminent English writers.

PHILIP: What do they want to do that for?

CELIA: I don't know. They've formed this organization called the Fellowship of Allied Terrorists Against Literature – F.A.T.A.L. It seems R. J. Morris was their first victim. But they've sent copies of this letter to twenty-four others saying they're going to kill them off, one by one.

PHILIP: How horrible!

CELIA: Yes. Anyway, Braham was transfixed by it.

PHILIP: Was he?

CELIA: He wasn't one of the twenty-five. He didn't know whether to be relieved or insulted.

PHILIP: Oh, I see.

(*Silence.*)

CELIA: He's asked me to go back and see him again this evening.

PHILIP: And will you?

CELIA: Certainly not. I wouldn't dream of it.

PHILIP: Come back, then. (*He smiles.*) All is forgiven.

CELIA: (*Bristling*) What do you mean?

PHILIP: I don't know. Joke, really.

CELIA: Oh.

PHILIP: But, I mean, I mean it.

CELIA: I've thought about it a lot.

PHILIP: I know . . .

CELIA: I've made up my mind.

PHILIP: Why?

CELIA: I think we'd probably make each other very unhappy.

PHILIP: Why?

CELIA: Because I don't think you'd be able to control me.

PHILIP: Does that matter?

CELIA: I didn't think so at first. In fact, to begin with, I thought that was the great advantage. But I don't any more.

PHILIP: Perhaps you're right.

CELIA: You see, that's the thing, you're so unassertive. Perhaps

55

you're right! Is that the best you can do?

PHILIP: All right, I'm not going to let you leave me!

CELIA: It's no good doing it now, is it, it's supposed to be spontaneous.

PHILIP: Well, I only said perhaps you're right because I was trying to look at it from your point of view. I mean, it's quite obvious what I see in you, isn't it? It's much more of a mystery what you see in me, and if you don't see what you did see any more, then perhaps you *are* right. If you see what I mean.

CELIA: No.

PHILIP: I'm not surprised you're having second thoughts, if all these people keep making passes at you all the time.

CELIA: What are you talking about?

PHILIP: Well, you know, Noakes and Johnson and all those people you were talking about last night.

CELIA: Oh, that.

PHILIP: Yes.

CELIA: None of that was true.

PHILIP: What?

CELIA: You know I'm always making things up.

PHILIP: Why?

CELIA: Well, you've got to say something, haven't you? Can't just sit there like a statue all evening. Like Liz. And lies are usually that much more interesting than the truth, that's all.

PHILIP: Oh. (*Pause.* PHILIP *considers this.*) Well, if that's the case, can't we try to come to some arrangement? I mean, I could try – or pretend – to be firmer, and you could pretend not to mind my weakness so much.

CELIA: No. Of course not.

PHILIP: Why not?

CELIA: What a monstrous suggestion.

PHILIP: Why?

CELIA: Well, it's . . . it's so deceitful. (PHILIP *laughs.*) No, look, it's different telling a few stories to liven up the party, from basing your whole life on a lie.

PHILIP: You just said lies were more interesting than the truth.

CELIA: You're being literal-minded again.

(*Silence.*)

PHILIP: I don't know. I've always been a failure with women.

CELIA: Oh, please.

PHILIP: But it's true. I remember, I remember the first girl I was ever in love with, Carol her name was, and I made the mistake, just as we were about to go to bed together for the first time, of telling her I was a virgin. Oh, well, then, she said, that was that, she wasn't going to be a guinea-pig for anyone. It was that phrase that did it. She became so entranced and horrified by the idea represented by her own quite fortuitous image, that I gave up, there was obviously no hope. Guinea-pig, 'I'm not going to be a guinea-pig', she kept on saying. So there it was. A whole relationship doomed by a random word-association. This is the same thing. You think I'm being sentimental and self-pitying just because I say I'm a failure with women. But I'm not. I'm just telling the simple truth, which is that I've never managed to give a woman satisfaction. I hope to. I hoped to with you. Given a bit of time. But in itself it's just a perfectly neutral fact. Like the fact I was a virgin when I was with Carol. (*He breaks off for a moment.*) She was very cruel. I adored her.

CELIA: You probably adored her because she was cruel.

PHILIP: On the contrary, it was when she became really cruel that I stopped adoring her. Your interpretation is both perverse and banal.

CELIA: Oh, don't be so pompous.

PHILIP: Sorry.

CELIA: You know something, you apologize far too often. You really oughtn't to, it's not very attractive.

PHILIP: Yes, I know, I'm sorry.

(CELIA *laughs, briefly, and* PHILIP *smiles as he realizes what he has said.*)

CELIA: What made you want to get married?

PHILIP: You.

CELIA: Yes, I know, but apart from that.

PHILIP: What do you mean?

57

CELIA: Well, you've been a comfortable bachelor for so long, I think you must have made some kind of abstract decision to get married, I mean quite apart from wanting to marry me.

PHILIP: I suppose that might be true.

CELIA: Well, why?

PHILIP: Perhaps it was because I'm beginning to get lonely.

CELIA: Go on.

PHILIP: I don't know, I've been doing this job for about twelve or thirteen years now, and I'm beginning to realize that I'm not immortal. Another thing is, when I sit and remember the past, you know, involuntary memories, what I remember most is certain rooms, rooms I've lived and worked in, at different times, in different countries. I was thinking about some of them the other day, and I suddenly realized something that had never occurred to me before. They were all empty. I mean I remember them as if I'm sitting in them, furniture, ceiling angles, street noises, clock ticking, all very vivid. But never anyone else. It gave me rather a shock.

CELIA: Don't you like being alone?

PHILIP: No, you know how gregarious I am. Look, who's the most boring person you know?

CELIA: I don't know. If you wait a few minutes, I could probably give you quite an impressive list.

PHILIP: Well, whoever it is, I'd quite willingly spend an hour a day with him for the rest of my life. Rather than being alone.

CELIA: Do you think you want to get married because you're unhappy?

PHILIP: I'm not unhappy. I mean, I am at the moment, but in general I've got no reason to be unhappy. In fact, I've got no right to be unhappy.

CELIA: That's never stopped anyone.

PHILIP: I know, I know that, but when you consider how pleasant my job is, how well-fed and privileged and comfortable I am and how easy it is for me to be tolerant and compassionate, it does seem perverse to be unhappy as well, doesn't it? I mean, to be unhappy on top of all that

58

does seem unreasonably self-indulgent, don't you think? It's not as if my life was a struggle. I sit in my study and read the latest journal, and occasionally I get up and change the record on my player, and sometimes I go abroad for a few weeks and wander round the galleries, and I play with words and make my anagrams and read the arts pages. And books, I must have read thousands of books, and seen hundreds of films and plays in my life. Not that many of them stay with me longer than an evening, but I'm grateful to all those people for whiling away my time. And that's all. Oh, yes, and I teach, and lecture, and write rather boring and pedantic articles, and from time to time, I suffer. Not often, I wouldn't like to exaggerate, but from time to time. A full life and an empty one.

(*He smiles.* CELIA *assesses this for a moment.*)

CELIA: Sympathy, is it, you're after?

PHILIP: Well, yes, perhaps, yes, I suppose so. I don't know. Perhaps not sympathy. Liking.

CELIA: At least you like everyone, that's half the battle anyway.

PHILIP: Yes, that's half the battle. The wrong half, but there we go.

CELIA: And you're an optimist, that makes life pleasanter, doesn't it?

PHILIP: I don't think I am. What makes you think that? You can like people without being an optimist. For instance, it's easier to like people if it occurs to you that they're going to die. It's difficult not to like a man if you can envisage his flesh falling from his bones.

CELIA: Oh dear, oh dear.

PHILIP: What?

CELIA: Let us grow amorous, you and I,
Knowing that both of us must die.

PHILIP: Who said that?

CELIA: Somebody must have.

(*Silence. Then, from the playing fields outside, a long, mournful whistle.*)

PHILIP: Full time.

CELIA: What?

59

PHILIP: Nothing.

CELIA: Not being lyrical, are you?

PHILIP: (*Shaking his head*) I . . .

CELIA: Let us eschew lyricism. Don't you think? I think lyricism should at all costs be eschewed.

PHILIP: Stop it.

CELIA: Well, you started it. I never realized you had a morbid streak in you.

PHILIP: Oh, yes, I suppose . . . (*He pauses, before deciding to go on with what he is saying.*) All my life, you know, I've been in a state of perpetual terror.

CELIA: Terror?

PHILIP: I think that's more accurate than the word I normally use for it, which is concern.

CELIA: What do you mean?

PHILIP: I mean, I mean that the basic feature of my character is an anxiety to please people and to do what they want, which leads to, that is, which amounts to a passion, and which is, in fact, so advanced that I can only describe it as . . . terror.

CELIA: In other words, it's not that you like people, it's just that you're afraid of them.

PHILIP: No, there's no contradiction in that, the one is a consequence of the other.

CELIA: I don't believe that.

(*Silence.*)

PHILIP: I'll tell you something I've never told anyone before, it's one of the most humiliating things that ever happened to me. When I was teaching in Hong Kong, I used to, walking from the lecture-hall to the car-park, I used to pass a hunchback, a, a cripple with an enormous head, who used to sit on the pavement and beg. After a time, I got into the habit of giving him a little money, every day, when I passed him. This went on for a bit, and then, to my great embarrassment, he started to clean my car. I tried to tell him not to bother one day when I found him at it, but he didn't understand, he just smiled and nodded and went on polishing, so I just left it, it seemed to be what he wanted to do. So every day, I would come out of my lecture, walk past him, press a little money into his hand, shamefully little, now I come to think of it, get into my beautiful, shiny car and drive off.

I used to keep a cache of small change handy to pay him, but one day, for some reason, I found I had none left, in fact, as I was leaving the building I found I had nothing smaller than a ten-dollar note, which was obviously, I thought to myself, far too much to give him. So, on this particular day I walked hurriedly past on the other side of the street, hoping he wouldn't see me, and crossed into the car-park as quickly as I could. But I'd just got into the car and put the key in the ignition, when I saw him hobbling towards the entrance of the car-park on his crutches at great speed, stopping occasionally to wave his duster at me. No, I thought, I can't face this, so I started up, and put my foot down, and raced out of the car-park. Now, I don't know about this, I mean, I'm sure I wasn't anywhere near him, but for some reason he panicked, and tried to jump backwards – and I just had this appalling glimpse of his crutches going up in the air as he overbalanced and fell on to his back. Needless to say, I didn't stop.

After that, whenever he saw me coming, he used to get up, move down the road a bit and go indoors. I hoped I'd be able to make it up with him, but I never got a chance, he never, he never let me get near him again.

No wonder they want our blood.

CELIA: Why are you telling me all this? I can't ever remember you talking so much.

PHILIP: I don't want you to go.

(*Silence.*)

CELIA: My problem is, all the men I fall in love with turn out to be such terrible people.

PHILIP: Oh. Do you think so?

CELIA: Not you, I don't mean you. That's what I'm trying to say. I was never really in love with you because you aren't firm enough. I don't think I'm capable of loving anyone as weak as you.

PHILIP: Do you prefer to be bullied then?

CELIA: I prefer to know where I stand.

(*Silence.*)

PHILIP: Can't we . . . isn't there. . . ?

CELIA: I don't think so.

PHILIP: Are you sure?

CELIA: Yes. Yes, now I've made up my mind, I honestly don't know what it is I ever saw in you.

PHILIP: Oh, well. Oh, well, then.

CELIA: No, don't misunderstand me. I'll always like you, I'll always be fond of you. It's just that we're not compatible.

PHILIP: So you already said. I still can't see it myself, but I suppose I shall just have to take your word for it.

CELIA: Now I think it would be best if I went.

(*She gets up.*)

PHILIP: Don't.

CELIA: Yes.

PHILIP: Please.

CELIA: I think it would be best.

PHILIP: Stay and talk to me. I feel a bit suicidal.

CELIA: Oh, don't exaggerate.

PHILIP: Well, you know. Stay and talk for a bit.

CELIA: Look, what have we got to talk about now? What could we possibly talk about?

PHILIP: Anything.

(CELIA *bursts into tears.* PHILIP *is amazed, he takes her in his arms and she sobs uncontrollably for a minute, then slowly recovers.*)

CELIA: Sorry.

PHILIP: Are you all right, love?

CELIA: Yes. All right now.

PHILIP: What's the matter?

CELIA: What do you think?

PHILIP: But I mean . . . I mean, it's your decision.

CELIA: What difference does that make?

PHILIP: All right, now, are you?

CELIA: Yes, thanks.

PHILIP: Would you like a glass of water or anything?

CELIA: No, no. I really must go now. Good-bye.

PHILIP: Good-bye. (*He takes her face in his hands and kisses her on the eyes and on the mouth.*) What now? Death, hell, destruction, madness, suicide, or will he come through smiling?

CELIA: Yes.

PHILIP: When will I see you again?

CELIA: Not for a bit. Not until we've got over it.

PHILIP: Soon.

CELIA: I expect so. (*She moves quickly to the door.*) Good-bye.
(CELIA *exits.*)

PHILIP: Good-bye, love.
(*He stands for a moment in the centre of the stage, disconsolate. Then he sits at his desk, picks up a book, and reads. He breaks off for a moment and stares into the distance, then returns to his book. He makes a note.*)
BLACKOUT
(*The second movement of Albinoni's Concerto in D minor for oboe and strings, Op. 9, No. 2.*)

SCENE SIX

A few hours later. Evening. PHILIP *is now writing a letter, apparently with some difficulty. After a time, he puts his pen down and thinks for a moment, gazing vacantly into space.*

PHILIP: But I . . . (*He breaks off, gets up, goes over to the bookshelf, takes down a book and looks something up.*) Yes.
But I was thinking of a plan
To dye one's whiskers green,
And always use so large a fan
That they could not be seen.
Yes. (*He smiles, then, after a short pause, moves over to the telephone and dials a two-figure number.*) Hello, Don? . . .
Yes . . . I wonder if you could just come round for a minute, I'd like to talk to you . . . Well, yes, it is, rather . . . it is, it's been a day of major catastrophes, and I . . . Well, in fact, I want to ask your advice about something . . . it won't take a minute, honestly . . . all right, thanks, right.
(PHILIP *crosses the room and pours himself a drink. A knock at the door and* DON *enters. He smiles at* PHILIP *and slumps into an armchair.*)

DON: Hello.

PHILIP: Scotch?

DON: Thanks.

PHILIP: Sorry to drag you over here. Are you busy?
(*He pours a drink for* DON, *takes it over to him.*)

DON: Well, no, not exactly, I . . . well, I'll tell you about it in a minute. First of all, what's your problem? You don't look very well.

PHILIP: I don't feel very well. I mean, I feel a bit remote.

64

DON: What do you mean?

PHILIP: Distant.

DON: Why? What's the matter?

PHILIP: Well, Celia came round this afternoon and told me she didn't want to marry me any more.

DON: Oh.

PHILIP: Last night, Araminta stayed here under circumstances too appalling to relate.

DON: Really?

PHILIP: And this morning Celia came round here before Araminta had left.

DON: Oh, I see.

PHILIP: No. Because Celia admitted that she'd decided to leave me anyway.

DON: Did she?

PHILIP: She having spent the night with Braham.

DON: (*Bewildered*) Good God.

PHILIP: Although she said that had nothing to do with it either.

DON: With what?

PHILIP: Her decision.

(*Silence.*)

DON: How extraordinary.

PHILIP: She said what you said when we were talking about it yesterday. She said she didn't think we were compatible.

DON: Meaningless nonsense.

PHILIP: But you said that as well.

DON: Yes. But I was speaking theoretically.

PHILIP: (*Uncomprehending*) Oh.

DON: You see, I always divide people into two groups. Those who live by what they know to be a lie, and those who live by what they believe, falsely, to be the truth. And having decided that Celia belonged to the first group and you to the second, I concluded that you weren't compatible, and that furthermore that was what attracted you to one another. But, I mean, trying to make elegant patterns out of people's hopelessness doesn't really work. It's only a frivolous game.

PHILIP: Seems to have worked on this occasion.

DON: What is wrong with the statement: 'all generalizations are false'?

PHILIP: It's a generalization.

DON: See, you're not as remote as all that.

PHILIP: But why . . . why do you say I live by what I believe, falsely, to be the truth?

DON: Because you do. Your whole behaviour is based on the assumption that everyone is like you.

PHILIP: Isn't everybody's?

DON: No. Of course not. Most people's behaviour is based on desperate hope that everyone isn't like them.

PHILIP: And why do you think Celia lives by a lie?

DON: Because her vanity demands it.

PHILIP: I'm not sure about that.

DON: I am.

PHILIP: Well, no doubt if you go on about it long enough, you'll persuade me to believe it. I haven't even got the courage of my lack of convictions.

DON: Oh, I wish I'd said that.

PHILIP: Why?

DON: I don't know, it sounds good.

PHILIP: That's not really why I said it, believe it or not.

DON: Sorry. I'm sorry.

(*Silence.*)

PHILIP: And which category do you belong to?

DON: What?

PHILIP: Of the two.

DON: Oh, I live by a lie. In my case, the lie is that I am a teacher of English, when in fact I am paid a handsome sum by the college to perfect a technique of idleness which I hope will eventually become unparalleled in academic history.

PHILIP: Oh, rubbish, you're not idle. You're famous for your conscientiousness.

DON: Ah, well, that's part of the art. I perform, in fact I sometimes actually volunteer for, all those little administrative tasks, which require no effort or application whatsoever and which can be done quite automatically. In that way, you see, I acquire a reputation for conscientiousness, and also provide myself with an excuse in the unlikely event that I should be caught out not knowing something I ought to know.

PHILIP: You're exaggerating.

DON: Oh, no, I'm not. In my youth I might have been concerned about my idleness, I used to make feeble attacks on it by doing things like setting my striking clock an hour fast, but I think I knew all along what I was heading for. When I struggled through my finals in that cunning and devious way, I think I knew this was my destination. I worked hard my first year teaching, my God, yes. I took a couple of dozen index cards and noted down ten points about each of the subjects that might reasonably be expected to come my way. And now, twenty-four weeks a year, I simply select the relevant card and give my pupils the points they've omitted in their essays, or if they've got them all I say, wonderful, see you next week, and I recover from this strenuous activity with twenty-eight weeks a year of total inactivity, usually in some pleasantly warm climate. I've given up all ideas of writing books, research, all that nonsense, I'm just settling, settling into my character. I am more than half in love with easeful sloth. I'm . . . what's that word that means bloodless?

PHILIP: Etiolated?

DON: Etiolated. That's it, etiolated. Only fit for lying about on a sofa with the curtains pulled, listening to baroque music and occasionally dabbing at the temples with a damp flannel. Do you know that I'm capable now of emptying my head completely for two or three hours at a stretch? Not a single thought of any kind. Nothing. That's not easily done, you know.

PHILIP: I'm sure.

DON: I think that if one manages in one's lifetime not only to come to terms with one's own uselessness but to begin actually enjoying it as well, that's something, don't you think, something, some kind of . . . an achievement.

PHILIP: Perhaps.

(Silence.)

DON: I'm sorry, Philip.

PHILIP: Why?

DON: It's typical of you, you know.

PHILIP: What?

DON: You've had the most terrible day, everything has gone wrong, you ask me round to give you some support or advice or something and all that happens is that I talk about myself.

PHILIP: That's all right.

DON: I'll shut up now. You tell me what you want. What can I do for you?

PHILIP: Well, when I was talking to Celia this afternoon, she asked me why I wanted to get married, I mean apart from wanting to marry her. It made me realize that she was right, that I did want to get married, that I was lonely, now that youthful hopes have faded in the usual way. I'm sorry, I didn't mean to get maudlin.

DON: No, go on. What is friendship, if not a chance to indulge in mutual self-pity?

PHILIP: And I was thinking what you said to me yesterday about Liz.

DON: (*Shiftily*) Oh?

PHILIP: Yes, you remember you were saying you thought she liked me, and that she would be more suitable for me than Celia.

DON: Well . . .

PHILIP: Anyway, I've just sat down to write to her, I thought I'd ask her out or something, ask her to lunch, and I just wanted to ask you what . . . (*He breaks off, surprised by* DON'*s obvious embarrassment.*) What's the matter?

DON: Well, Liz is, she's in my room now.

PHILIP: Is she?

DON: She's been there since yesterday evening.

PHILIP: Oh. Oh, that's . . . erm . . .

DON: So I . . .

PHILIP: Yes. Yes.

DON: I've rather, you know, rather fallen for her.

PHILIP: Oh, well, that's, er, isn't it?

DON: Yes.

PHILIP: I'm surprised, I didn't think you . . .

DON: I'm surprised, too, in fact, I'm amazed. She's such a quiet girl, I mean, you don't expect her to be, I mean, it just sort of happened, and then for her to be, well, so passionate, I was very surprised.

PHILIP: Yes.

DON: I'm sorry, Philip, it's just the way things happen . . .

PHILIP: That's all right.

DON: The last thing . . .

PHILIP: That's all right. Perhaps you should be going back to her now.

DON: No, it's all right.

PHILIP: I'd rather you did.

DON: No, look, you're just a bit upset . . .

PHILIP: Will you please get out!

DON: Oh, all right, if you . . .

PHILIP: Please go away!

(DON *exits uncertainly.* PHILIP *sits for a moment. Then he drains his drink, gets up, moves to his desk, crumples up the letter and throws it into the waste-paper basket. Next he moves back to the table, takes a cigarette from the cigarette-box and puts it in his mouth. Pause. Then he returns to the desk, opens a drawer and takes out a small pistol. He considers it for a moment, then puts it down on the desk. He lifts the telephone and dials two figures.*)

Hello, Don? . . . I'm sorry about all that . . . yes, I just, you know, well, I am sorry anyway . . . What? . . . Now? All right, if you're sure that's all right . . . are you sure? . . . Yes, I am quite hungry . . . well, that's very kind . . . yes, I'm all right, now . . . no, don't let's get sentimental about it . . . well, anyway, I'm about to do something terrible . . . you'll see in a minute . . . I forgot to tell you, I thought of a new anagram today . . . 'imagine the theatre as real' . . . 'imagine the theatre as real' . . . it's an anagram for 'I hate thee, sterile anagram' . . . Yes, I thought so too . . . all right, then . . . yes . . . yes . . . see you both in a minute.

(*He hangs up, pauses a moment, then picks up the pistol. He*

turns it toward him and pulls the trigger. A small flame springs from the hammer. PHILIP *lights his cigarette from it, inhales deeply, pockets the pistol and exits, leaving the door open.*)
(*Aria: 'Ich freue mich auf meinen Tod' from Bach's Cantata No. 82, 'Ich habe genug'.*)
CURTAIN

TOTAL ECLIPSE

For Harry and Lynn
and in memory of work and friendship
with Robert Kidd and Victor Henry

This new production of *Total Eclipse* opened at the Lyric Theatre, Hammersmith on 5th May 1981. The cast was as follows:

PAUL VERLAINE	Simon Callow
MME MAUTÉ DE FLEURVILLE	Eileen Page
MATHILDE VERLAINE	Lynsey Baxter
ARTHUR RIMBAUD	Hilton McRae
M. MAUTÉ DE FLEURVILLE	Tim Seely
CHARLES CROS	William Sleigh
ÉTIENNE CARJAT	Tim Seely
JEAN AICARD	Peter McKriel
JUDGE THÉODORE T'SERSTEVENS	Tim Seely
CLERK	Peter McKriel
EUGÉNIE KRANTZ	Judith Barker
BARMAN	William Sleigh
ISABELLE RIMBAUD	Anna Nyghe

Directed by David Hare
Designed by Hayden Griffin

The first performance of *Total Eclipse* was given at the Royal Court Theatre on 11th September 1968. The cast was as follows:

MME MAUTÉ DE FLEURVILLE, Verlaine's mother-in-law	Kathleen Byron
MATHILDE VERLAINE, Verlaine's wife	Michele Dotrice
ARTHUR RIMBAUD	Victor Henry
PAUL VERLAINE	John Grillo
CHARLES CROS	Malcolm Ingram
M. MAUTÉ DE FLEURVILLE	Nigel Hawthorne
ÉTIENNE CARJAT	Nigel Hawthorne
ERNEST CABANER	William Hayland
JEAN AICARD	Stanley Lebor
CLERK	Stanley Lebor
JUDGE THÉODORE T'SERSTEVENS	Nigel Hawthorne
EUGÉNIE KRANTZ	Ursula Smith
ISABELLE RIMBAUD, Rimbaud's sister	Gillian Martell
A BARMAN	William Hoyland
MAID	Judy Liebert

Artists, customers in cafés etc.

Directed by Robert Kidd
Designed by Patrick Procktor

ACT ONE

SCENE ONE

VERLAINE'S VOICE: Sometimes he speaks, in a kind of dialect, of the death which causes repentance, of the unhappy men who certainly exist, of painful tasks and heart-rendering departures. In the hovels where we got drunk, he wept looking at those who surrounded us, the cattle of poverty. He lifted up drunks in the black streets. He had the pity a bad mother has for small children. He moved with the grace of a little girl at catechism. He pretended to know about everything, business, art, medicine. I followed him, I had to!

(*During this, the lights go up on the drawing-room/conservatory of the Paris home of the* MAUTÉS DE FLEURVILLE *at 14, Rue Nicolet. It's the 10th September, 1871. Indications of discreet affluence.* MME MAUTÉ DE FLEURVILLE, *a handsome middle-aged woman, is trimming flowers and handing them to her daughter,* MATHILDE VERLAINE, *who arranges them in a vase.* MATHILDE *is an attractive girl of 18, now 8 months pregnant.*

The women continue working for a moment in silence; then, a strange, incongruous figure enters the room and stands for a moment, waiting in the shadows, watching them. Neither of them notices him. He is ARTHUR RIMBAUD. *His appearance is striking. He is not quite 17 and looks his age. His hands are large and dirty. His tie hangs loose round his neck like a piece of old string. His trousers are too short and end an inch above his blue socks. His boots are filthy. He's extremely good-looking: thin lips, cold, grey eyes. Eventually he speaks, startling the women considerably.*)

RIMBAUD: Evening. I'm looking for M. Paul Verlaine.
MME M. DE F.: Are you . . . M. Rimbaud?
RIMBAUD: Yes.
MME M. DE F.: Oh, M. Rimbaud, I am Mme Mauté de Fleurville,

M. Verlaine's mother-in-law. And this is Mme Verlaine, my
daughter.

(RIMBAUD *smiles frostily, nodding to the two women.*)

MME M. DE F.: You're not with M. Verlaine?

RIMBAUD: No.

MME M. DE F.: Only he went to the station to meet you. I suppose
he must have missed you.

RIMBAUD: Yes, well he doesn't know what I look like, does he?

MME M. DE F.: Er, how did you get here?

RIMBAUD: Walked.

(*Silence.*)

MME M. DE F.: Perhaps . . . would you like a wash?

RIMBAUD (*considers this a moment*): No thanks.

MME M. DE F.: Did you give your luggage to one of the servants?

RIMBAUD: I didn't meet any servants.

MME M. DE F.: Well, then, it's in the hall, is it?

RIMBAUD: What?

MME M. DE F.: Your luggage.

RIMBAUD: I haven't got any luggage.

MME M. DE F.: No . . . luggage?

RIMBAUD: No.

MME M. DE F.: Oh.

(*Silence.*)

MATHILDE: Won't you sit down, M. Rimbaud?

(RIMBAUD *does so, slouching back in the chair and reaching
into his pocket to find a repulsive old clay pipe and some
matches. He lights the pipe, sucking noisily.*)

RIMBAUD: Mind if I smoke?

MME M. DE F. (*with obvious distaste*): Not at all.

(*Silence.*)

M. Verlaine and I were very impressed by your
poetry.

RIMBAUD: He let you read it?

MME M. DE F.: Oh yes, I'm a fervent admirer of the Muse. We're
great friends with M. Victor Hugo, you know. He's an
utterly charming gentleman.

RIMBAUD: He's getting a bit senile.

MME M. DE F.: I don't think so. He still has perfect command of his faculties. Naturally to the young he seems a little elderly. But then the young must always be revolutionary.

MATHILDE: You're even younger than we thought you were.

RIMBAUD: Oh, yes?

MATHILDE: How old are you?

MME M. DE F.: Darling, it's not very polite to ask people their ages.

MATHILDE: I'm sorry. I was just so interested.

(RIMBAUD, *ignoring this exchange, has risen and crossed to the window. He stands, looking out at the garden.*)

RIMBAUD: Pleasant view.

MME M. DE F.: Yes, charming, isn't it?

RIMBAUD: Pleasant.

(RIMBAUD *picks up a china animal, considers it with distaste, puts it down and turns back to the window. At this moment,* PAUL VERLAINE *hurries in. He's 27, bearded, but already going bald. He's well-dressed and looks like a civil servant with private means—which is what he is. He doesn't at first notice* RIMBAUD.)

VERLAINE: I combed the station but no sign of him.

RIMBAUD (*without turning round*): He's here.

VERLAINE: M. Rimbaud?

(*He advances towards* RIMBAUD, *hand outstretched, then, as* RIMBAUD *turns towards him, hesitates for a moment, apparently transfixed by* RIMBAUD's *appearance.*)

RIMBAUD: M. Verlaine.

(*They shake hands.*)

VERLAINE: You found your own way here. What initiative.

MME M. DE F.: Good, well, I must see about organizing some dinner. I expect M. Rimbaud must be hungry.

RIMBAUD: Starving.

MME M. DE F.: Yes. (*To* MATHILDE.) Come along, dear. You can give me a hand and the men can have a little chat.

(*She leaves with* MATHILDE.)

VERLAINE: Well, this is . . .

(RIMBAUD *nods.*)

VERLAINE: How old are you, if you don't mind my asking?

RIMBAUD: I do.

VERLAINE: Oh, sorry.

RIMBAUD: Sixteen.

VERLAINE: Sixteen? Are you sure?

RIMBAUD: Of course I'm sure.

VERLAINE: It's just that in your letter you said you were twenty-one.

RIMBAUD: You never want to believe what I say in my letters.

VERLAINE: I'm amazed. I thought those poems you sent me were remarkable for someone of twenty-one. For someone of sixteen, they're—unprecedented.

RIMBAUD: That's why I told you I was twenty-one. I didn't want you to feel patronizing before you'd read them.

VERLAINE: Of course, it all becomes clearer now. The fact that your mother kept you at home with no money. If you're sixteen. You've left school, have you?

RIMBAUD: Yes.

VERLAINE: I suppose your mother must be very angry with me.

RIMBAUD: No, once she found out you'd sent me my train fare, she seemed quite happy.

VERLAINE: I'm sorry I wasn't there to meet you at the station. The thing is, your train arrived at the emerald hour. The hour of absinthe. (*He grins, gesturing at the room.*) I don't suppose this is quite what you expected. My wife and I did have a flat on the Quai de la Tournelle when I was working. But what with one political upheaval and another I decided I was too sensitive for the Civil Service. So I couldn't afford to keep on the flat. Then Mathilde's father, rot his guts, very generously offered us a floor of this house. I thought it might be a good idea, Mathilde being pregnant and everything.

RIMBAUD: And wasn't it?

VERLAINE: Yes, yes, except for my loathsome father-in-law. Fortunately for you, he's away at the moment. On a shooting party. Where I sincerely hope he will meet with a fatal accident. My daily devotions are entirely directed to that end. (*He sighs.*) I suffered for that girl, you know. I had to wait over a year before I could marry her. The fates were against it. It was delayed so many times. By pestilence and

80

war. Literally. She caught smallpox at the last minute. I thought, Mary mother, have I waited all this time to get married to a flayed hedgehog? Fortunately she was quite unmarked. Two days before the wedding one of my best friends committed suicide. Then, the next day, the final indignity, I got called up. But I was immune to all the portents. I even squirmed out of that—and I married her.

It's just that being pregnant's had a bad effect on her. She's only a child.

RIMBAUD. So am I.

(MME MAUTÉ DE FLEURVILLE *comes in with* MATHILDE, *who crosses to* VERLAINE *and kisses him on the cheek. Then she smiles at* RIMBAUD, *who doesn't respond, but fills and relights his pipe.*)

MME M. DE F.: Dinner's almost ready.

RIMBAUD: Good, I'm famished.

(*Silence.*)

MME M. DE F.: You come from the Ardennes, don't you, M. Rimbaud? Charleville?

RIMBAUD: Yes.

MME M. DE F.: Pleasant town, Charleville, isn't it?

RIMBAUD: The last place on God's earth.

MATHILDE: And what does your father do?

RIMBAUD: Drinks mostly, I believe. We haven't seen him for ten years.

MATHILDE: I'm sorry.

RIMBAUD: No need to be. He's very well out of it.

(*Silence.*)

MME M. DE F.: Perhaps you'd like to read something to us after dinner?

RIMBAUD: I don't think so.

MATEILDE: Oh, why not?

RIMBAUD: I don't want to.

MME M. DE F.: M. Rimbaud's probably tired, dear.

RIMBAUD: No. I never read out my poetry.

MATHILDE: Oh, but all the other poets do it. We have soirées here and . . .

RIMBAUD: I'm not interested in what all the other poets do.

VERLAINE: Don't you think poets can learn from one another?

RIMBAUD: Only if they're bad poets.

MATHILDE: I'm sure you'd enjoy our soirées. We had a lovely one last week. Poetry and music. Musset and Chopin.

RIMBAUD: Musset?

MATHILDE: Yes. Don't you like Musset? He's my favourite poet. Except for Paul, of course. Daddy was at school with him.

RIMBAUD: Slovenly facile rubbish. The most objectionable and least talented of all the miserable buffoons of this dreary century. A poet for schoolboys and women.

VERLAINE: Ah, but what about his plays?

RIMBAUD: The theatre is beneath contempt.

VERLAINE: Your opinions are firm.

RIMBAUD: Shouldn't they be?

(*Silence.*)

Listen, I must have a piss. Can you tell me where it is?

(VERLAINE *leads him across the room, murmuring directions. Then, when* RIMBAUD *has left, he turns back to the others.*)

MME M. DE F.: Well.

MATHILDE: He's not how I imagined him.

VERLAINE: He's all right.

CURTAIN

SCENE TWO

The same; 25th September, 1871.

RIMBAUD *walks into the empty room, smoking his pipe. He looks round the room, then, after a moment's consideration, goes over and picks up the china animal we have already seen him handle in Scene 1. He contemplates it briefly, then deliberately drops it on the floor and smashes it. He's moving away, back towards the door, when* M. MAUTÉ DE FLEURVILLE *appears. He's an imposing man of 64, with a white beard. He's startled to see* RIMBAUD, *who by contrast, seems remarkably calm.*

RIMBAUD (*hospitably*): Morning. Everyone's out, I'm afraid. They should be back soon. Unless you've come to see the old boy.

M. DE F.: The old boy?

RIMBAUD: M. Mauté de Fleurville. You're not a friend of his, are you?

M. DE F.: Er . . . no.

RIMBAUD: No, I didn't think you were. As far as I can gather he doesn't have any friends.

M. DE F. (*faintly*): Really.

RIMBAUD: Yes. Apparently he defeats all comers with an impregnable combination of tediousness and avarice. It is darkly rumoured that he cannot resist rifling the pockets of those who fall stunned by the monotony of his anecdotes. (M. DE F. *is beginning to show signs of impending fury. He utters one or two indeterminate sounds, but* RIMBAUD *interrupts him, suavely changing tack.*) You wouldn't like to buy a crucifix by any chance, would you? (*He produces one from an inside pocket.*) Because I happen to have one with me which I can let you have on extremely reasonable terms. It's ivory, I think. (M. DE F. *stares at the crucifix, which he recognizes as his own, with rage and incomprehension.*) Tempted?

M. DE F.: Who the hell are you?

RIMBAUD: I might ask you the same question. Except I'd be more polite.

M. DE F.: I am Mauté de Fleurville.

RIMBAUD: Morning.

(*He exits smartly.* M. DE F. *gapes after him. Then he hurries out the other side of the room. Hiatus.* VERLAINE *and* MATHILDE *appear, the former looking considerably more rumpled than in the first scene and already somewhat drunk.*)

VERLAINE: All I'm saying is, if he goes, I go.

MATHILDE: That's just silly.

VERLAINE: We can't just put him out on the street, he's only a boy.

MATHILDE: He's met all your friends. One of them will give him a bed for a while.

(*She sits down on the chaise longue and puts her feet up,
grunting slightly with the effort.*)

VERLAINE: People don't understand him. I'm the only one who
understands him.

MATHILDE: Well, Daddy certainly won't understand him.

VERLAINE: I'm tired of being ordered about by that old bastard.
He has no sympathy at all for my position. None of you
seem to realize we had a revolution this year, which I
supported. I could have been shot. If I hadn't been thrown
out of my job, do you suppose I'd have accepted his bloody
charity for one moment?

MATHILDE: No, but it's . . .

VERLAINE: I've been very tolerant with him, but this time I'm
putting my foot down. Now do I make myself clear?

MATHILDE: Yes.

VERLAINE: And you're going to give me your full support?

MATHILDE: Yes.

VERLAINE: I know you, the minute he comes back, you'll start
agreeing with him.

MATHILDE: No. I won't.

VERLAINE: It's not asking much, for God's sake, all I'm doing is
helping a friend. I don't know why we have to go through
all this. I'm your husband.

MATHILDE: I'm sorry, Paul.

VERLAINE: Are you trying to annoy me?

MATHILDE: No.

VERLAINE: Well, don't.

(*Silence.*)

MATHILDE: Why is it you like him so much?

(*Silence.* RIMBAUD *slips into the room. He looks cheerful.*)

RIMBAUD: I'm off.

VERLAINE: No, look, you don't have to go. We're going to have it
out with him when he gets back.

RIMBAUD: He's back.

VERLAINE: What?

RIMBAUD: We met. I don't think he's best pleased.

VERLAINE: Did he ask who you were?

RIMBAUD: It wasn't that kind of conversation.

VERLAINE: Well, look, we've decided you must stay. (*To* MATHILDE.) Haven't we?

MATHILDE (*hesitates fractionally*): Yes.

RIMBAUD: It doesn't matter.

VERLAINE: Of course it matters. Why should we let the old sod treat us like this?

RIMBAUD: It's his house.

VERLAINE: Right, well, I'm going to say either we all stay or we all leave together, what about that?

(RIMBAUD *smiles at* MATHILDE, *a touch ironically.*)

RIMBAUD: Suits me.

VERLAINE: I mean, what could he do?

MATHILDE: He could cut off our allowance.

RIMBAUD: Ah.

VERLAINE: He wouldn't do that. Yes he would. Well, what the hell, eh, don't you think?

RIMBAUD: It's entirely up to you.

VERLAINE: Look, why don't we discuss this over a few drinks? Then . . . er . . . I mean, look, go down and order one up for me, I'll join you in a minute. Actually . . .

RIMBAUD: What?

VERLAINE: I do know someone who has a spare room going. What's the joke?

RIMBAUD: Nothing.

VERLAINE: Listen, if you'd rather . . .

RIMBAUD: No, no. I'll go and order you a drink. (*He starts moving towards the door, then stops, turns back and produces a piece of paper out of his pocket.*) I've got a list here of the books I want from Mauté's library, I thought you might nick them for me, not all at once, one by one will do. They'll obviously be more use to me than they are to him. (*He hands the list to* VERLAINE. *As he does so,* M. DE F. *sweeps into the room followed by* MME DE F. *He's about to speak, but falls silent when he sees* RIMBAUD. *Silence.* RIMBAUD *grins.*)

RIMBAUD (*to* VERLAINE): Don't be long.

(*He leaves, bowing to the* MAUTÉS. *Silence.*)

M. DE F.: Since when have you had the right to invite people to stay here without my permission?

VERLAINE: Since you had the kindness to offer the second floor of your house to Mathilde and me, I've treated it as our home.

M. DE F.: So it is, your home, not a guest house.

VERLAINE: If I can't put up one guest in my home when I feel like it, I might as well live somewhere else.

M. DE F.: If you weren't so idle, you might be able to afford to.

VERLAINE: Now, listen, you know very well, that since the Commune . . .

M. DE F.: Any excuse.

VERLAINE: I don't notice you working your fingers to the bone.

M. DE F.: Now look here, Verlaine, I want that hooligan out of my house. Is that clear?

VERLAINE (*roars at him*): He's already left!

(*Silence.*)

M. DE F.: And when you see him next, you'll kindly ask him to return all the objects he's pilfered.

VERLAINE: What are you talking about?

M. DE F.: I'd hardly stepped in the door when he tried to sell me one of my own crucifixes. (*To his wife.*) Come along, dear.

MME M. DE F.: I think perhaps I'd better stay and have a word with them.

M. DE F.: Will you come with me!

(*Cowed by his tone,* MME M. DE F. *follows her husband out of the room.* VERLAINE *is still furious.*)

MATHILDE: You'd better get him to give back Daddy's crucifix.

VERLAINE: What?

MATHILDE: You must get it back from him.

VERLAINE: I've no intention of doing anything of the sort. If your father's capable of throwing that boy out without a penny he deserves to lose more than a few religious knick-knacks. He's got no right to have Christ hanging all over his walls. You people don't understand what poverty is. Do you realize that in Charleville, whenever Rimbaud wanted a book, he had to go and steal it off the bookstall.

MATHILDE: That proves what sort of a person he is.

(VERLAINE *bounds across the room, seizes* MATHILDE *by the ankles and drags her off the chaise longue. She crashes heavily*

86

*to the floor. He stands over her as she struggles to her feet,
then punches her hard in the face. She goes over again,
bringing down a small table as she falls. Brief silence. She
moans softly.* VERLAINE *starts forward and lifts her off the
floor.*)

VERLAINE: I'm sorry . . . I'm sorry, love . . . sorry. You
    shouldn't have said that. (*He helps her over towards the
    chaise longue.*)

    (M. *and* MME M. DE F. *hurry in.*)

M. DE F.: What's going on? (*Silence.*) Mm?

MATHILDE: Nothing.

M. DE F.: What was all that noise then?

MATHILDE: I . . . knocked the table over.

MME M. DE F.: Are you all right, dear?

    (MATHILDE *nods, very pale.* M. DE F. *turns to*
    VERLAINE, *and speaks in venomous undertones.*)

M. DE F.: There's nothing more contemptible than a man who
    maltreats a woman.

VERLAINE: Unless it be a man who maltreats two.

    (*He storms out.*)

CURTAIN

SCENE THREE

A small attic room in the Rue de Buci.
RIMBAUD *is lying on a divan and* VERLAINE *is sitting in an armchair.*

VERLAINE: You see, I didn't think it really mattered who I
    married. I thought anybody would do. Anybody within
    reason.

RIMBAUD: I don't know why you wanted to get married in the
    first place.

VERLAINE: I was tired of it all. I was living with Mother then.
    Only because I was too lazy to live by myself and look
    after myself. She did everything—and to an extent it was

all right. I did what I liked and only went home to sleep or to eat or to change. But in the end it began to wear me down, the office was so boring and home was so boring, and I started to drink more and more and I had to keep slipping off to the brothel, things got worse and worse. Day after day I'd wake up fully clothed, covered with mud or with all the skin off my knuckles, feeling sick and nursing a dim memory of $3\frac{1}{2}$ minutes with some horrible tart who hadn't even bothered to take her shoes off.

This can't go on, I said.

It has to stop.

One day I went round to see Sivry, who was doing the music for a farce I was going to write and as he was showing me up to his room we passed through the Mautés' main room, you know, and there she was, standing with her back to us, looking out of the window. I think we startled her because she turned round very quickly. I was stunned, she was so beautiful. She was wearing a grey and green dress and she stood in the window with the sun going down behind her. Sivry said, had I met his half-sister, Mathilde, and I said, no, unfortunately I hadn't. So he introduced me and said I was a poet and she smiled and said how nice, she was very fond of poets.

I tell you, that was it.

A week later, I was in Arras, I woke up in bed with the most grisly scrubber you can imagine, sweaty she was, snoring, I was trying to tiptoe away when she woke up and called me back.

I went back.

Later on that morning I wrote to Sivry and told him I wanted to marry Mathilde.

I thought she was ideal. Plenty of money. Well enough brought up to have all the wifely virtues. Innocent. Beautiful. Sixteen. She would look after me. And be there every night in my bed.

I had to wait over a year before I could have her. It was agony. Delicious. I used to go there every evening and look at her. When the wedding was put off for the third time, I practically went berserk. And when it finally took place, I couldn't believe it. I felt giddy all day.

The next few months were marvellous, you know. I didn't care about the war, the Prussians could do what they liked as far as I was concerned. I was otherwise engaged. I can't tell you how wonderful it was. It was a kind of legalized corruption. She was impossibly coy at first, she didn't like it, she didn't understand it, it hurt. And then slowly she began to take to it, she relaxed, she became . . . inventive. And then one night, when I was very tired, she suggested it.

(*Silence.*)

RIMBAUD: And now you have a son.

VERLAINE: And now I have a son.

(*Silence.*)

RIMBAUD: What happened last night, anyway?

VERLAINE: Well, I . . . can't remember it very clearly. As you know I wasn't quite myself when I left you last night. My idea was to go to bed with her, as I think I mentioned to you.

RIMBAUD: Many times.

VERLAINE: Yes, well I thought, it's a week since the child was born, it ought to be all right by now. I said I'd be careful, but, I mean, it's been such a long time. Anyway, it was no good, she wouldn't.

RIMBAUD: So what happened?

VERLAINE: I don't know, God knows.

RIMBAUD: Did you hit her again?

VERLAINE: No, no, not this time. I woke up, as in Arras, with my boots on the pillow, and tiptoed away. But she didn't call me back.

RIMBAUD: So you're still frustrated?

(VERLAINE *nods. Silence.*)

RIMBAUD: Why don't you leave her?

VERLAINE: What?

RIMBAUD: Leave her.

VERLAINE: Why?

RIMBAUD: Because she's no good to you.

89

VERLAINE: What do you mean?

RIMBAUD: Do you love her?

VERLAINE: Yes, I suppose so.

RIMBAUD: Have you got anything in common with her?

VERLAINE: No.

RIMBAUD: Is she intelligent?

VERLAINE: No.

RIMBAUD: Does she understand you?

VERLAINE: No.

RIMBAUD: So the only thing she can give you is sex?

VERLAINE: Well. . . .

RIMBAUD: Can't you find anyone else?

VERLAINE: I. . . .

RIMBAUD: You're not that fussy, are you?

VERLAINE: No.

RIMBAUD: Anyone within reason would do, wouldn't they?

VERLAINE: Within reason.

RIMBAUD: What about me?

(*Silence.* RIMBAUD *laughs.*)

RIMBAUD: Are you a poet?

(*Silence.* VERLAINE *smiles uneasily.*)

VERLAINE (*cautiously*): Yes.

RIMBAUD: I'd say not.

VERLAINE: Why?

RIMBAUD: Well, I hope you wouldn't describe that last volume of pre-marital junk as poetry?

VERLAINE: I most certainly would. Very beautiful love poetry, that is.

RIMBAUD: But you've just admitted that all you wanted to do was to go to bed with her.

VERLAINE: That doesn't make the poems any less beautiful.

RIMBAUD: Doesn't it? Doesn't it matter that they're lies?

VERLAINE: They're not lies. I love her.

RIMBAUD: Love?

VERLAINE: Yes.

RIMBAUD: No such thing.

VERLAINE: What do you mean?

RIMBAUD: I mean it doesn't exist. Self-interest exists. Attachment based on personal gain exists. Complacency exists. But not love. It has to be re-invented.

VERLAINE: You're wrong.

RIMBAUD: Well, all right, if you care to describe what binds families and married couples together as love rather than stupidity or selfishness or fear, then we'll say that love does exist. In which case it's useless, it doesn't help. It's for cowards.

VERLAINE: You're wrong.

RIMBAUD: When I was in Paris in February this year, when everything was in a state of chaos, I was staying the night in a barracks and I was sexually assaulted by four drunken soldiers. I didn't like it at the time, but when I got back to Charleville, thinking about it, I began to realize how valuable it had been to me. It clarified things in my mind which had been vague. It gave my imagination textures. And I understood that what I needed, to be the first poet of this century, the first poet since Racine or since the Greeks, was to experience everything in my body. I knew what it was like to be a model pupil, top of the class, now I wanted to disgust them instead of pleasing them. I knew what it was like to take communion, I wanted to take drugs. I knew what it was like to be chaste, I wanted perversions. It was no longer enough for me to be one person, I decided to be everyone. I decided to be a genius. I decided to be Christ. I decided to originate the future.

The fact that I often regarded my ambition as ludicrous and pathetic pleased me, it was what I wanted, contrast, conflict inside my head, that was good. While other writers looked at themselves in the mirror, accepted what they saw, and jotted it down, I liked to see a mirror in the mirror, so that I could turn round whenever I felt like it and always find endless vistas of myself.

However, what I say is immaterial, it's what I write that counts.

If you help me, I'll help you.

VERLAINE: How can I help you?

RIMBAUD: By leaving your wife. As far as I can see, it's the only hope there is for you. Not only are you unhappy as you are, it's not even doing you any good. What are you going to do, write domestic poetry for the rest of your life? Bringing up baby? Epics of the Civil Service? Or will you be forced, you, Verlaine, to write impersonal poetry? Foolish plays and feeble historical reconstructions? If you leave her and come with me, both of us will benefit. And when we've got as much from one another as we can, we split up and move on. You could even go back to your wife again.

It's just a suggestion, it's up to you.

VERLAINE: You seem to forget that I have a son now.

RIMBAUD: On the contrary, that's what makes it so ideal. If you leave your wife now, you won't be leaving her alone. She can spend all her time bringing up her son. That's what my father did, he just upped and left us one day, he couldn't have done a wiser thing. Except he'd left it a bit late.

VERLAINE: But how would we live?

RIMBAUD: You've got some money, haven't you?

VERLAINE: Ah, now I understand. I help you by supporting you, and you help me by renewing my rusty old inspiration. Is that it?

RIMBAUD: Not altogether.

VERLAINE: Well, how else are you going to help me, then?

RIMBAUD: You name it.

(*Long silence.*)

CURTAIN

SCENE FOUR

The Café du Théâtre du Bobino; 20th December, 1871.
A dinner of the Vilains Bonshommes, a poetry society. Five of the guests are visible to the audience, arranged in such a way as to suggest a much larger gathering. At one end, although placed as if in the centre of the table, is the featured poet, JEAN AICARD, *a portly and respectable figure, now somewhat nervously sorting through his papers. Next to*

him is ÉTIENNE CARJAT, *43, a dapper figure with a goatee, who is talking to* CHARLES CROS, *29, a languid dandy with frizzy hair and a lugubrious moustache. Next to* CROS *is* VERLAINE, *somewhat the worse for drink and, next to him,* RIMBAUD, *slouched back in his chair and wearing a battered top hat. The scene opens with two simultaneous conversations: between* CROS *and* CARJAT *and between* RIMBAUD *and* VERLAINE. *In addition, there's the buzz of general chatter.*

CROS: The principle is very much like photography. Only instead of photographing a man's face, you photograph his voice. Then twenty years later, just as you might open the photograph album, you simply put the relevant cylinder into the paleophone and listen to him reading his poem or singing his song.

CARJAT: And you think you could invent a machine like that which worked?

CROS: Perfectly possible.

CARJAT: Why don't you get on with it then?

CROS: I don't know. I can't be bothered with all the organization and effort.

CARJAT: You're an idle bugger.

CROS: I'm a man of ideas.

RIMBAUD: For Christ's sake, let get the fuck out of here.

VERLAINE: We can't, he's just about to start reading.

RIMBAUD: Who?

VERLAINE: Aicard. Just there.

RIMBAUD: I don't think I'm going to like his stuff much.

VERLAINE: You won't, it's dreadful. Best we can hope for is get a bit of sleep while he's at it.

RIMBAUD: And another drink. (*He calls offstage.*) Oy! Any chance of another drink?

CARJAT: What about your colour photographs? How are you doing with them?

CROS: There's no money in it.

CARJAT (*leaning across to* RIMBAUD): Are you interested in photography?

RIMBAUD: No.

CARJAT: Only I was wondering how you'd like to be

photographed.

RIMBAUD: Not particularly.

CARJAT: Because I'd like to photograph you. I find your appearance very striking. You have a very fine bone structure.

RIMBAUD: Really?

CARJAT: Yes. I don't think much of your poetry, but I love your bone structure.

RIMBAUD: Why don't you think much of my poetry?

CARJAT: Well, it's very promising of course. But it seems to me that all that ingenuity is rather marred by . . . well, not exactly a juvenile urge to shock, but something of that sort.

RIMBAUD: And were you shocked when you read it?

CARJAT: No, I . . . no, of course not.

RIMBAUD: Then why should you suppose that I intended you to be?

CARJAT: Well . . . that's not really the point.

VERLAINE: Seems fair enough to me.

CARJAT: I . . . I could object to your technical approach.

RIMBAUD: I could object to your tie.

CARJAT: Well, if you're going to take that attitude. . . .

VERLAINE: He doesn't like discussing his poetry.

CARJAT: I see.

CROS: I don't think you're being quite fair to the boy. I like his work. Especially that one about the girl spending the night before her first communion in the lavatory with a candle. My word. Magnificent stuff.

RIMBAUD (*coldly*): Thank you.

(*There is now a general ripple of applause, as* AICARD *rises to his feet.* CROS *and* CARJAT *applaud,* VERLAINE *and* RIMBAUD *do not.* CROS *then turns away from* RIMBAUD *and murmurs to* CARJAT, *as* AICARD *begins speaking.*)

AICARD: Thank you very much, gentlemen. I should like to start by reading a poem from a collection I am planning for children.

(*As he continues to speak,* RIMBAUD *fetches a small phial out of his waistcoat pocket and empties the contents into* CROS's *beer, which immediately begins to bubble and fizz.*)

94

I would ask you to bear in mind that the poem is written expressly for children, although, as with all worthwhile work for children, it is hoped that what is said is not entirely without relevance to adults.

(CROS *turns back to the table, reaches for his beer, lifts it almost to his lips, then does a horrified double-take and puts the glass down hurriedly. He speaks to* RIMBAUD *in an urgent whisper.*)

CROS: What have you put in it?

RIMBAUD: Sulphuric acid.

CROS: What?

AICARD (*simultaneously*): The poem is called "Green Absinthe" (*He clears his throat.*) "Green Absinthe".

(CROS, *appalled, continues to stare at* RIMBAUD, *but the latter has turned his attention to* AICARD, *and bursts into ironic applause.*)

"Green absinthe is the potion of the damned. . . ."

(RIMBAUD *belches.*)

"A deadly poison silting up the veins,
While wife and child sit weeping in their slum. . . ."

RIMBAUD (*distinctly*): I don't believe it.

(*A certain sensation.* AICARD *soldiers on.*)

AICARD: "The drunkard pours absinthe into his brains."

RIMBAUD: Shit.

AICARD: "Oh! Drunkard, most contemptible of men. . . ."

RIMBAUD: Shit.

AICARD (*his voice cracking*): "Degraded, fallen, sinful and obtuse. . . ."

RIMBAUD: It is! Authentic shit!

AICARD: "Degraded, fallen, sinful and obtuse
You scruple not to beat your wife and child. . . ."

RIMBAUD: For trying to deprive you of the juice.

(*Pandemonium. Protests, laughter, shouting.* CARJAT *springs to his feet.*)

CARJAT: Get out, you!

(*Silence falls.*)

RIMBAUD: Me?

CARJAT: Yes you, you offensive little bastard. Get out, or I'll throw you out. Who the hell do you think you are?

RIMBAUD: I think I may, may I not, be permitted to raise some objection against the butchering of French poetry?

CARJAT: No. You may not. Now apologize and get out.

(*He moves towards* RIMBAUD, *who rises and grips* VERLAINE's *sword-stick.*)

VERLAINE: Careful.

RIMBAUD (*to* CARJAT. *Grim and pale*): Don't come any nearer.

CARJAT: If you think you can frighten me with that thing. . . .

(RIMBAUD *draws the sword.*)

(*ends weekly*): . . . you've got another think coming.

RIMBAUD (*almost a whisper*): Don't come any nearer.

(*Deadlock. They watch each other venomously. Then* CARJAT *attacks, and* RIMBAUD *slashes out at him.* CARJAT *stops, appalled, cries out, grasps his wrist. Blood flows. Chaos.*)

VERLAINE: Careful, I said.

RIMBAUD (*turning to* AICARD, *with a great roar*): And now, you.

(*He bears down on* AICARD, *who, for a moment is transfixed with horror, before breaking and running for his life.*)

Miserable poetaster!

(*He pursues* AICARD *round the room.*)

Fucking inkpisser!

(*He slashes wildly at* AICARD *who manages to get the table between himself and* RIMBAUD. *Meanwhile* RIMBAUD *is resisting all attempts to disarm him by laying about him at anyone who comes too close.*)

In the days of François Premier, wise and benevolent giants roamed the countryside. And one, let me tell you, one of their . . . natural functions was to rid the world of pedants, fools and writers of no talent . . . (*he leaps up on to the table*) by . . . by pissing on them from a great height, and . . . and. . . .

(*At this point he passes out, crashing spectacularly to the ground.* VERLAINE *and* CROS *seize him and hurry out with him.*)

CURTAIN

The Café du Rat Mort; 29th June, 1872.

The café is fairly empty. VERLAINE *and* RIMBAUD *sit at a table, drinking absinthe. Throughout the scene,* RIMBAUD's *behaviour is curious and distant, as if he has been taking hashish or drinking all night. Occasionally he shakes off this air of drugged or drunken fatigue for a time, only to relapse into dreamy contemplation when, for instance,* VERLAINE *speaks at any length.*

RIMBAUD: The first thing he did, it seems, when he was given the ring, a magic ring you understand, was to summon up a beautiful woman, the most beautiful he could imagine. And they were wonderfully happy and lived alone on a light blue southern island. Then one day he explained to her that with the ring he could grant her anything she wanted, and she asked him to build her a city. So he caused a city to grow up out of the sea, full of churches and echoing courtyards, and quite empty. She was so delighted with it that he granted her another wish, and she asked for a ship. So he gave her a magnificent galleon which needed no crew to look after the silk hangings and golden figurehead. It seemed to give her such happiness that he decided to grant her one more wish. "One more wish," he said. "I will grant you one more wish."

"Give me the ring," she said.

He gave it to her. She smiled serenely at him and threw it into the sea. At once she disappeared, the ship disappeared, and the city slowly sank back under the water.

For a long time after that the man sat looking out to sea without moving. Finally he began to weep because he understood what he had done and that he would be alone for ever.

That was it. Something like that.

Colour is what's missing, colour. That's what this gives

you, thick colours you can smell and hear. Otherwise
everything is grey and dull. I want to go somewhere I can
get it without this. South. Away from the dusty mantel-
piece of Europe. If I may so express myself. (*He chuckles.*)

Let's leave. I've always wanted to see the sea. We can't
possibly go on as we are. Can we? I mean. . . . I mean,
let's leave.

God, my hands are cold.

Can't we leave?

VERLAINE: Here?

RIMBAUD: Paris, Paris.

VERLAINE: Well. . . .

RIMBAUD: We certainly can't go on as we are. It's been dragging
on for months as it is. You can't keep sending me home
whenever she threatens a divorce and summoning me back
when the coast looks clear. What's needed, if . . . (*he
blinks, concentrates*) if I may use a crude term I know you
find distasteful, is a decision.

VERLAINE: Ah, decisions. . . .

RIMBAUD: Yes.

VERLAINE: I always say, show me a decisive man and I'll show
you a fool.

RIMBAUD: Wishful thinking.

VERLAINE: Anyway, she's not very well at the moment.

RIMBAUD: I'm not surprised, if you keep setting fire to her.

VERLAINE (*indignantly*): I haven't set fire to her since May.

(*They both laugh.*)

VERLAINE: It's not very funny.

(*They both laugh some more.*)

RIMBAUD: It's pathetic. (*He stops laughing, abruptly.*) Pathetic.
Your acts of violence are always curiously disgusting.

VERLAINE: What do you mean?

RIMBAUD: They're not clean. You're always in a drunken stupor
when you commit them. You beat up Mathilde, or hit me,
or throw your son against the wall—and then you start
apologizing and grovelling.

VERLAINE: I don't like hurting people.

RIMBAUD: Then don't. And if you do, do it coolly, and don't

insult your victim by feeling sorry for him afterwards.

(*Silence.*)

VERLAINE: I don't think I ever told you about the most terrible of my little tantrums—when I attacked my brother and sisters.

RIMBAUD: I didn't think you had any.

VERLAINE: Oh, yes. Like you, I have one brother and two sisters, The difference between mine and yours is that mine are dead.

My mother had three miscarriages before I was born— and being of a rather morbid turn of mind, she kept the results in a cupboard in the bedroom, preserved, ominously enough, in alcohol. There they were, Nicolas, Stéphanie, and Élisa, stacked away on the top shelf in three enormous jars. I'll never forget the first time I came across them, when I was a small boy. I was fooling around in the bedroom, burrowing in the cupboard, which I'd never dared do before, when I saw these great jars. The light was pretty bad and I couldn't make out what was in them at first, so I got a chair and stood on it. I suddenly saw these three little puckered people, lined up, staring at me in a strangely knowing way.

I had no idea what they were. I dimly associated them with preserved plums, and for weeks after that my stomach turned over whenever we had roast.

When I found out they were my own flesh and blood, they assumed a monumental importance in my life. I used to watch Mother dusting them every Thursday, and consult them on all matters of moment. Not that they were very helpful. They remained expressionless and inscrutable at all times, and as the years wore on, I began to detect a certain superciliousness in their attitude, a kind of amused contempt for their younger brother, which came to be very wounding.

The older I got, the more I resented them.

They had a right to be complacent, I thought, because they'd had it very easy and didn't know any better. But they had no right to despise me for being less fortunate than they were. When Mother told me how difficult and dangerous my birth had been, I often felt there had been some terrible mistake and that my place was up there with them in a large glass jar, meditating quietly and being dusted on Thursdays. "If any of you had lived," I used to tell them, "I wouldn't have had to. So it's all your fault." They looked back at me, smug, sceptical and unblinking. And I envied their peace.

One night only a couple of years ago, I got very drunk indeed. I was really at the bottom of the pit, things couldn't have been blacker. As happens from time to time, I had a nasty attack of the vomits, racking out blood and bits and all the accumulated muck I'd been pouring into myself for years, I wished I was dead, you know how it is, the worst. That's when I get violent. When I see things as they really are.

I went to the cupboard and looked at Nicolas, Stéphanie and Élisa, sitting there comfortably, wise and gloating. And lifted my stick and smashed the jars.

(*Silence.*)

RIMBAUD: And?

VERLAINE: I remember being saturated in alcohol—and a glimpse of them grotesquely marooned in their broken jars before I passed out. The next day when I looked, they were back, just as before, in identical jars, and Mother never said a word about it. Were it not for the fact that I surprised a look of active dislike on their faces when I next visited them, I'd be inclined to write off the whole incident as a ghastly dream.

RIMBAUD: Few corpses can have led such eventful lives.

(VERLAINE *laughs, summons the waiter.*)

VERLAINE: Two.

(*Silence.*)

RIMBAUD: You have digressed. Strayed from the point.

VERLAINE: We have all day and all night to get back to it. Whatever it was. Is.

RIMBAUD: It's time to leave.

VERLAINE: I've just ordered another drink.

RIMBAUD: Paris.

VERLAINE: Oh.

RIMBAUD: This is the time to go, the summer. We will be
children of the sun and live in pagan pleasure. (*He smiles.*)
The happiest times of my life were when I ran away from
home. Walking through fields in the sun, or sheltering in a
wood, sleeping under hedges, ham sandwich and a beer for
supper, I just carried on until I had no money left, and
even then it didn't seem to matter. I've never known such
long and coloured days. Only I never got far enough. I
wanted to follow a river to the sea, or walk to Africa and
cross a desert. I wanted heat and violence of landscape.

But what I didn't have on those days often added to their
harmony.

VERLAINE (*a trace of irony*): It sounds idyllic.

RIMBAUD: It was. Much more idyllic than that filthy little room
where I sleep when you're making love to Mathilde, and
don't sleep when you're making love to me.

VERLAINE: You do sleep. I often watch you sleeping.

RIMBAUD: You often wake me up. (*Pause.*) Isn't it time you left
Mathilde?

VERLAINE: Why? I love her.

RIMBAUD: You can't possibly.

VERLAINE: I love her body.

RIMBAUD: There are other bodies.

VERLAINE: That's not the point. I love Mathilde's body.

RIMBAUD: But not her soul?

VERLAINE: I think it's less important to love the soul than to
love the body. After all, the soul may be immortal, we have
plenty of time for the soul: but flesh rots.
(RIMBAUD *laughs.*)

VERLAINE: Do you find that amusing?

RIMBAUD: Not really.

VERLAINE: If people laugh at flesh it is because they do not love
its textures, or its shape and smell, as I do. Or its sadness.

RIMBAUD (*coldly*): Quite possibly.

VERLAINE: It is my love of flesh which makes me faithful.

RIMBAUD: Faithful? What do you mean?

VERLAINE: It's possible to be faithful to more than one person. I'm faithful to all my lovers, because once I love them, I will always love them. And when I am alone in the evening or the early morning, I close my eyes and celebrate them all.

RIMBAUD: That's not faithfulness, it's nostalgia. If you don't want to leave Mathilde, it's not because you're faithful, it's because you're weak.

VERLAINE: If strength involves brutality, I prefer to be weak.

RIMBAUD: With you, weakness involves brutality as well. (*Pause.*) Don't expect me to be faithful to you.

VERLAINE: I don't.

(*Silence.*)

RIMBAUD: I'm leaving Paris next week. You can come with me or not, as you like.

VERLAINE: Where are you going?

RIMBAUD: I don't know. Just away. Are you coming?

VERLAINE: I. . . .

RIMBAUD: Or are you staying with Mathilde?

VERLAINE: I don't know. The thought of losing either of you is unbearable. I don't know. Why are you so harsh with me?

RIMBAUD: Because you need it.

VERLAINE: Why? Isn't it enough for you to know that I love you more than I've ever loved anyone, and that I always will love you?

RIMBAUD: Shut up, you snivelling drunk.

VERLAINE: Tell me if you love me.

RIMBAUD: Oh, for God's sake. . . .

VERLAINE: Please.

(*Silence.*)

Please. It's important to me.

RIMBAUD: Why?

VERLAINE: Please.

(*Silence.*)

RIMBAUD: I . . . you know I'm very fond of you . . . we've been very happy sometimes . . . I. . . .

(*A very long silence.* RIMBAUD *blushes deeply. He produces a large knife from his pocket, and picks at the table with it.*)

102

(*Almost inaudibly*): Do you love me?

VERLAINE: What?

RIMBAUD: Do you love me?

VERLAINE (*puzzled*): Yes.

RIMBAUD: Then put your hands on the table.

VERLAINE: What?

RIMBAUD: Put your hands on the table.

(VERLAINE *does so.*)

Palm upwards.

(VERLAINE *turns his hands palm upwards.* RIMBAUD *looks at them for a moment, and then with short, brutal hacks, stabs at both of them.* VERLAINE *sits looking at his hands in amazement, as blood begins to drip down on to the floor.*)

The only unbearable thing is that nothing is unbearable.

(VERLAINE *stares uncomprehendingly at him, then gets up and stumbles out of the café.* RIMBAUD *watches him leave, then gets up himself and hurries out after him.*)

CURTAIN

SCENE SIX

A room in the Hôtel Liégeois, Brussels; 22nd July, 1872.

VERLAINE *is lying half-in and half-on the rumpled bed.* MATHILDE *stands with her back to the audience, getting dressed.*

VERLAINE: That was wonderful, darling.

(*Silence.*)

VERLAINE: Wonderful.

MATHILDE: Can you pass me my stockings? (*She indicates the chair by the bed, where they are neatly arranged.*)

VERLAINE: Why don't you come and lie down and relax for a bit? You don't have to get dressed right away, do you?

MATHILDE: It's getting late.

VERLAINE: Nonsense, it's only about half-past eight.

MATHILDE: Someone might come.

VERLAINE: Who?

MATHILDE: Mummy.

VERLAINE: I thought you weren't meeting her till lunch. Anyway, we're married aren't we, for God's sake?

(MATHILDE *walks over to the chair, picks up her stockings, sits down on the bed, and starts to put them on.*)

Do you remember . . .

(*He leans forward and strokes her hair, then turns her face to him and kisses her. She submits briefly, and, it seems, without enthusiasm to his embrace.*)

. . . happier times?

MATHILDE: Yes. (*She continues dressing.*) Are you coming back to Paris with me?

VERLAINE: I . . . don't know.

MATHILDE: Why don't you want to?

VERLAINE: I do want to, it's just . . . it's just I don't think it's safe in Paris any more. I mean . . . I mean they're still arresting people connected with the Commune. Look what happened to Sivry. Four months in jail for practically no reason at all. And who gave him his job? I did. I had a very important job, you know. I was virtually in charge of the propaganda press.

MATHILDE: I know, but that was over a year ago.

VERLAINE: The police are slow, but methodical. They don't forgive and forget. I couldn't stand going to jail. (*Pause.*) That's why I think it's better if I play it safe and stay out of the country for a few months.

MATHILDE: With Rimbaud.

VERLAINE: Well. . . .

MATHILDE: I suppose he's wanted by the police too.

VERLAINE: Er. . . .

MATHILDE: Why don't you want to come back?

VERLAINE: I. . . .

MATHILDE: Why do you prefer him to me?

VERLAINE: I don't love, I don't. (*Pause.*) It's just . . . I'll tell you what it is. I can't stand living with your parents any more. I will not be pushed around by that stupid old man. I can't understand what makes you want to stay there.

MATHILDE: Because . . . because it's not safe anywhere else.

VERLAINE: What do you mean?

MATHILDE: You know what I mean.

(*Silence.*)

VERLAINE: It's only when I've been drinking, dear. It's only when I'm drunk, and it all becomes too much for me. It's only when things are impossible. You know I don't mean it.

MATHILDE: At the time you mean it.

(*Silence.*)

MATHILDE: You know . . . you know Daddy wants me to get a divorce?

VERLAINE: I've told you before. . . .

MATHILDE: He says if you go away with Rimbaud, you're deserting me and I can get a divorce. He says. . . .

VERLAINE (*shouting*): It's nothing to do with him. It's me you're married to, not him. (*More calmly.*) Do you want a divorce?

MATHILDE: No. (*She begins to cry soundlessly, her body shaking with sobs.*)

VERLAINE: Don't cry, love. (*He puts his arms round her, and soothes her.*) That's better.

MATHILDE: Are you going to come with me?

VERLAINE: I don't know, love, I. . . .

MATHILDE: Not home, I don't mean home, I mean abroad.

VERLAINE: Abroad?

MATHILDE: Yes, I had this idea, I thought of this idea, don't be angry. I thought we might . . . emigrate. To . . . Canada

VERLAINE: Canada?

MATHILDE: Or New Caledonia. There are quite a lot of our friends out there, you know, Rochefort and Louise Michel, and I thought, as you said you wanted to write a book about the Commune, they might be able to help. And I've heard it's lovely out there, the country and the forests, and we could try again.

VERLAINE: What about the baby?

MATHILDE: Well, that's up to you, but I thought, if you wanted to that is, we could leave him behind, I mean, Mummy would be only too pleased to look after him for a couple of years, or however long . . . we wanted to stay.

VERLAINE: It's a nice idea. . . .

MATHILDE: It's the best thing we could do, Paul. You could
write, and be quiet, and . . . and it'd be like it was when we
were first married, and. . . .

VERLAINE: What?

MATHILDE: Doesn't matter.

VERLAINE: No, go on.

MATHILDE: Well, I . . . was only going to say you could stop
. . . it would be easy for you . . . if you wanted to . . . stop
drinking.

VERLAINE: You're frightened of me, aren't you?

(MATHILDE *doesn't answer*, VERLAINE *puts his arms round her
again.*)

I do love you, you know. (*He kisses her.*) Don't think I like
getting drunk. I mean I do like getting drunk, but I don't
like being drunk. Or anyway . . . when I hit you or . . . do
any of the things I do, I feel so terrible about it the next
day, the only thing I can think of is to get drunk again and
forget about it. I can't stop, there's no end to it. I'm not
angry with you, when you mention it. Most of the time I
want to give it up as much as you want me to. But it's as
difficult as deciding to wake up when you're asleep.

Perhaps I could wake up out there. That's what I want
most, you know, it's what I really want most. I want to live
quietly, and work hard and well, and make love to you, and
have children, would that be possible do you think? It
should be easy, do you think it's possible?

MATHILDE: Yes, it's possible.

VERLAINE: Can you see us, can you see us living in a log cabin, or
whatever they have?

MATHILDE: Why not?

VERLAINE: Then let's go, for Christ's sake, let's go. Before it's
too late.

MATHILDE: We can go whenever you like.

VERLAINE: God, I love you.

(*He kisses her again, a long, clinging kiss, at the end of which
he begins to undress her. She pulls away from him.*)

MATHILDE: No, not now.

VERLAINE: Why not?

(*She doesn't answer, attending to her clothes.* VERLAINE *sits up and touches her shoulder.*)

VERLAINE: Come on.

MATHILDE: No.

VERLAINE: Why not?

MATHILDE: I'm very tired. I've been in the train all night, and I didn't sleep very well.

VERLAINE: Please.

MATHILDE: Look, I'm supposed to be meeting Mummy for breakfast, and I'm late already. Why don't you get dressed and come with me?

VERLAINE: I don't want breakfast, I want you.

MATHILDE: There'll be other times.

VERLAINE: Will there?

MATHILDE: Well, of course. Help me with this, will you?

(VERLAINE *helps her into her stern, billowing dress.*)

VERLAINE: What's this meeting Mummy for breakfast?

MATHILDE: I promised to. I think she hopes you'll come too.

VERLAINE: Tell her I don't feel like breakfast today.

MATHILDE: Can I tell her it's all right about Canada

VERLAINE: What's it got to do with her?

MATHILDE: Well, she's got to be told, hasn't she?

VERLAINE: Now?

MATHILDE: Well, it *is* all right, isn't it?

VERLAINE: I . . . don't know.

MATHILDE: But, you just said. . . .

VERLAINE: I know, I know what I said.

(*Silence.*)

MATHILDE: If it's money you're worrying about, Daddy's already said he'll pay the fare. . . . (*She stops dead, realizing that she has made a bad mistake.*)

VERLAINE: What?

MATHILDE: Nothing.

VERLAINE: What did you say?

MATHILDE: Nothing.

VERLAINE: Go on, you'd better go and have breakfast. You can tell her it's all right.

MATHILDE: Can I really?

VERLAINE: Yes.

MATHILDE: That's wonderful.

VERLAINE: Here. Give us a kiss.

(*She does so.*)

Now, off you go.

MATHILDE: 'Bye.

VERLAINE: Good-bye.

(*Exit* MATHILDE. VERLAINE *gets dressed, sunk in reflection. Suddenly* RIMBAUD *walks in. He takes in the situation at a glance.*)

RIMBAUD: I see.

VERLAINE: What are you doing here?

RIMBAUD: Nice, was it? A scene of conjugal bliss? I thought she looked a bit flushed.

VERLAINE: How did you get here?

RIMBAUD: I waited until she came down, and went up.

VERLAINE: How did you know which room?

RIMBAUD: I was with you when you booked it.

VERLAINE: Oh, yes.

(*Silence.*)

RIMBAUD: Well, aren't you going to tell me all about it? You don't usually spare me the hideous details. What about those thighs, paradoxically both moist and silken? What recondite position did you adopt this time?

VERLAINE: I think you'd better go.

RIMBAUD: Oh, I will. I'm more interested in what the position is than in what it was. Just explain it to me, and then I'll go.

VERLAINE: Well, look, not here, she might come back. Let's. . . .

RIMBAUD: No. I want to hear it from you now, and I want you honest and I want you sober. The alternatives are simple. Either you stay in Brussels with me, in which case you send Mathilde back to Paris. Or you go back to Paris with Mathilde, in which case you will kindly leave me some money so that I can get back to France if I want to. That's all. Choose.

(*Silence.*)
Choose.

VERLAINE: I'm going back to Paris with Mathilde.

RIMBAUD: Right. (*He moves over to the door.*)

VERLAINE: Wait. Wait a minute. Give me a chance to explain.

RIMBAUD: Why should I? I don't need an explanation. I'm not going to waste my time trying to dissuade you, if that's what you want. It's your decision, you made it.

VERLAINE: Listen, don't go. I just want to explain it to you. Sit down a minute.

(RIMBAUD *remains standing, but moves a little nearer to the centre of the stage.*)

RIMBAUD: She might come back.

VERLAINE: Never mind that. It doesn't matter.

(RIMBAUD *smiles and slumps into a chair.*)

Well, she . . . she suggested that we emigrate. To Canada

RIMBAUD: Did she?

VERLAINE: Yes.

RIMBAUD: Ah.

VERLAINE: Don't you think it's a good idea.

RIMBAUD: No

VERLAINE: Why not? What difference does it make?

Look, it's a chance for me. We've got friends out there, it'd be a quiet life, I could write and relax and stop drinking. . . .

RIMBAUD: Leave behind all the bad influences of Europe. . . .

VERLAINE (*after a pause*): Yes. Enjoy the country. . . .

RIMBAUD: Clean living. Back to Rousseau. The noble savage. Paul and Mathilde and their dog Fidèle. Man against the elements. Her idea, was it?

VERLAINE: Yes.

RIMBAUD: Or Daddy's? Nefarious Daddy's?

VERLAINE: You don't care about my happiness, do you?

RIMBAUD: No, and neither should you.

(*Silence.*)

VERLAINE: I know I said I'd send her back. But you've never been able to understand how much I love her. She's so beautiful. I came in, this morning, I walked in without knocking and she was lying there, naked, on the bed. She looked so beautiful, when I came in she looked so young and confused. . . .

(*He breaks off.* RIMBAUD *is laughing helplessly.*)

VERLAINE: What's the matter?

RIMBAUD: Was she really lying naked on the bed when you arrived?

VERLAINE: Yes.

RIMBAUD: I like that, that's marvellous.

VERLAINE: What do you mean?

RIMBAUD: My estimation for her goes up a long way.

VERLAINE: Why?

RIMBAUD: For realizing what was required, and providing it.

VERLAINE: You are a cynical bastard. She was resting after the journey. She didn't know what time I was arriving.

RIMBAUD: Is she in the habit of lying about the place with no clothes on?

VERLAINE: No. (*Pause.*) Look, what does it matter, anyway?

RIMBAUD: It doesn't. (*Pause.*) She's your wife, you love her, go back to her. (*He gets up.*)

VERLAINE: Christ, I don't know what to do.

(*Silence.* RIMBAUD *begins moving towards the door.*)
What do you think?

RIMBAUD: I think it's time I went. I think it's up to you.

VERLAINE: God.

RIMBAUD: I shall await your decision in the hotel.

VERLAINE: Don't go.

RIMBAUD (*smiles*): Perhaps a few drinks would make the whole situation seem a bit clearer.

(*Exit* RIMBAUD. *The light fades on* VERLAINE, *who sits, staring morosely in front of him.*)

CURTAIN

ACT TWO

SCENE ONE

VERLAINE'S VOICE: How many night hours have I watched beside his dear sleeping body, wondering why he wanted so much to escape from reality. There never was a man with such an aim. I could see—let alone the effect on him—that he might be a serious danger to society. Did he perhaps know secrets *to change life*? No, he's only looking for them, I told myself. His kindness is enchanted. I am its prisoner.

(*During this the lights go up on a large Georgian room converted into a bed-sitting room at 34–5 Howland Street, London; 24th November, 1872.*

VERLAINE *is sitting at the table, writing a letter.* RIMBAUD *is lying on or in the bed, reading, jotting down the odd note in an exercise book. The conversation is disjointed and sporadic, the atmosphere domestic.*)

RIMBAUD: What's your greatest fear?
VERLAINE: Mm?
RIMBAUD: I said what's your greatest fear?
VERLAINE: I don't know. I wouldn't like to mislay my balls. (*He continues writing.*) Why, what's yours?
RIMBAUD: That other people will see me as I see them.
(*Silence.*)
RIMBAUD: What time is it they open?
VERLAINE: Not till one o'clock. Ludicrous bloody country.
RIMBAUD: I hate Sundays.
VERLAINE: Nothing but warm beer you have to drink standing up. What is it makes them so bloody respectable? Even the beggars have shiny shoes.
RIMBAUD: I've always hated Sundays. Even in Charleville I

hated them. We used to march off to High Mass, like a . . . crocodile of penguins. First, Vitalie and Isabelle. Then, Frédéric and I. And bringing up the rear, Mother Rimbaud, the mouth of darkness. People used to point us out. She made us hold hands.

I've always felt, contrary to all evidence, that about five o'clock on Sunday evening must have been the time Christ died.

(*Silence.*)

VERLAINE: Chuck us a pear.

(RIMBAUD *does so.*)

Shall I give Lepelletier your love?

RIMBAUD: No.

(*Silence.*)

I love this language. "To put a spurt on",
"to lick the dust", "to test the bottom of a dog".
What do you suppose that means?

VERLAINE: It's what they have to do before they make their, what's it called, ox-tail soup. (*He picks up a bit of paper, reads.*) "William George of Castle Street offers a large and varied selection of French letters." Are we going to listen to George Odger this afternoon?

RIMBAUD: Who?

VERLAINE: George Odger, republican. (*He reads from a leaflet.*) ". . . will speak at Hyde Park on behalf of the discharged and imprisoned constables."

RIMBAUD: Doesn't sound very interesting to me.

VERLAINE: At least it's free.

(*Silence.* RIMBAUD *lights his pipe.*)

We're very short at the moment, you know.

RIMBAUD: So you keep saying.

VERLAINE: Don't you think it's time we took a job.

RIMBAUD: I've told you before, I'm not going to take a job. I've got better things to do with my time.

VERLAINE: I mean just a part-time teaching job or something?

RIMBAUD: No. There's nothing to stop you getting a job if you want to.

VERLAINE: I don't want to, I have to.

112

RIMBAUD: Well, I don't have to. Anyway . . . I'm not staying here much longer.

VERLAINE: Really?

RIMBAUD: It's best if I leave you for a bit.

VERLAINE: Why?

RIMBAUD: Look, do you want a divorce from Mathilde or not?

VERLAINE: Of course not.

RIMBAUD: Well, you're going to get one. They can give her one on desertion, you know, let alone desertion and sodomy.

VERLAINE: I know that.

RIMBAUD: I don't want to get mixed up in it.

VERLAINE: That's why it's better if you stay here. I mean, if you leave now, it'll be an admission of guilt, won't it? Obviously. The only answer is to bluff it out.

That's why I've told Lepelletier that if Mathilde's father likes we're ready to submit to a medical examination.

RIMBAUD: Are you mad?

VERLAINE: No, look, I've phrased it delicately. . . .

RIMBAUD: What have you said?

VERLAINE (*reads from the letter*): Rimbaud and I are quite prepared, if necessary, to let the whole gang of them look up our arses.

RIMBAUD: Suppose he takes you up on it?

VERLAINE: He won't.

RIMBAUD: I'm leaving next week.

VERLAINE: He couldn't possibly.

RIMBAUD: You don't think he made this accusation because he was looking for a way to liven up the long winter evenings, do you? He made it because he knows.

VERLAINE: Nonsense, it was a theatrical gesture.

RIMBAUD: You always judge people from a literary standpoint, which means that your assessment of their motives is usually inaccurate.

VERLAINE: Anyway, it's him that's in the wrong. How many times have I asked for my things back from that house, and he's still got them there.

RIMBAUD: You're in the wrong.

VERLAINE (*suddenly coldly angry*): All right, I'm in the wrong, if

113

you say so, then that's established, isn't it? Now perhaps
you'll let me get on and finish my letter.
(*Silence.* VERLAINE *writes for a while.*)

RIMBAUD: I shall leave next week.

VERLAINE: We'll discuss it later, shall we?

RIMBAUD: I doubt it.

(VERLAINE *signs his letter with a flourish.*)

VERLAINE: Course it won't go today, even if I post it. The post
is terrible in this country.

RIMBAUD: Are they open yet?

VERLAINE: Are we going to listen to Mr. Odger?

RIMBAUD: Drinks first.

VERLAINE: Just a minute, I must line my stomach first. (*He
pours himself a glass of milk and drinks.*) Ugh. It's horrible.
Want some?
(RIMBAUD *shakes his head.* VERLAINE *goes over to the window.*)
It's foggy. (*He puts on his overcoat, then wraps his long red
scarf carefully round his mouth.*) The old nosebleed. (*He stuffs
cotton wool in his ears and speaks as he does so, his voice
muffled by his scarf.*) One evening, I set out to assassinate
Napoléon III. I was rather drunk and I decided things had
gone far enough. Unfortunately I never managed it.
(*They smile at each other with some tenderness.*)

CURTAIN

SCENE TWO

8, Great College Street, London; 2nd July, 1873.
Drabber, anonymous bed-sitter. VERLAINE *is opening a bottle of
wine,* RIMBAUD *is lying on his bed, doing nothing.*

VERLAINE: Any chance of you moving about at all today?

RIMBAUD: I've always liked the autumn.

VERLAINE: It's supposed to be summer. Not that you can tell the
difference in England.

114

RIMBAUD: How long have we been in this hole?

VERLAINE: Not more than five weeks.

RIMBAUD: God, life will never end.

(VERLAINE *pours wine into two glasses and takes one over to* RIMBAUD.)

VERLAINE: A lot can happen in five weeks.

RIMBAUD: A lot can happen in ten minutes. But it rarely does.

VERLAINE: When I got married . . .

RIMBAUD: I thought you weren't going to mention that again.

VERLAINE: I was only. . . .

RIMBAUD: Well, don't.

VERLAINE: I'm sorry.

RIMBAUD: More.

(VERLAINE *goes over and pours him out some more wine.*)

VERLAINE: There have been good times, though, haven't there? I mean, we have been happy.

RIMBAUD: When?

VERLAINE: You know. Even you must grudgingly admit we've been happy sometimes.

RIMBAUD: I've told you before, I'm too intelligent to be happy.

VERLAINE: I remember you telling me once, when we were trying to get some sleep in a ditch in Belgium, that you'd never been so happy in your life.

RIMBAUD: Kindly spare us another bout of your lying and utterly revolting nostalgia.

VERLAINE: Why do you take such pleasure in being unhappy?

RIMBAUD: I assure you I get no more pleasure from pain than I do from pleasure.

VERLAINE: You've become perversely addicted to pessimism.

RIMBAUD: More.

VERLAINE: Get it yourself.

RIMBAUD: You're getting a bit assertive in your old age.

(*He gets up to pour himself some more wine.* VERLAINE *wanders over to the window.*)

VERLAINE: It's still raining.

(*Silence.*)

You're right about old age. I shall be thirty next birthday. Thirty. What a horrible thought.

RIMBAUD: Disgusting.

VERLAINE: And you're getting on. Nearly nineteen.

RIMBAUD: I begin to despair.

VERLAINE: Why?

RIMBAUD: When I was young and golden and infallible, I saw the future with some clarity. I saw the failings of my predecessors and saw, I thought, how they could be avoided. I knew it would be difficult, but I thought that all I needed was experience, and I could turn myself into the philosopher's stone, and create new colours and new flowers, new languages and a new God, and everything to gold. Thou shalt, I said to myself, adopting the appropriate apocalyptic style, be reviled and persecuted as any prophet, but at the last thou shalt prevail.

But before long I realized it was impossible to be a doubting prophet. If you are a prophet you may be optimistic or pessimistic as the fancy takes you, but you may never be anything less than certain. And I found I had tormented myself and poked among my entrails to discover something that people do not believe, or do not wish to believe, or would be foolish to believe. And with the lyricism of self-pity, I turned to the mirror and said Lord, what shall I do, for there is no love in the world and no hope, and I can do nothing about it, God, I can do no more than you have done, and I am in Hell.

Not that I haven't said all this before.

I have, and clearly a new code is called for. And in these last few weeks when you may have been thinking, I've just been lying here in a state of paralysed sloth, you've actually been quite right. But bubbling beneath the surface and rising slowly through the layers of indifference has been a new system. Harden up. Reject romanticism. Abandon rhetoric. Get it right.

And now I've got it right and seen where my attempt to conquer the world has led me.

VERLAINE: Where?

RIMBAUD: Here. My search for universal experience has led me here. To lead an idle, pointless life of poverty, as the minion of a bald, ugly, ageing, drunken lyric poet, who clings on to me because his wife won't take him back. (*Silence. At first* VERLAINE *is too astonished to speak.*)

VERLAINE: How can you bring yourself to say a thing like that?

RIMBAUD: It's easy. It's the truth. You're here, living like this, because you have to be. It's your life. Drink and sex and a kind of complacent melancholy and enough money to soak yourself oblivious every night. That's your limit. But I'm here because I choose to be.

VERLAINE: Oh yes?

RIMBAUD: Yes.

VERLAINE: And why exactly?

RIMBAUD: What do you mean, why?

VERLAINE: Why exactly did you choose to come back to London with me? What was the intellectual basis of your choice?

RIMBAUD: This is a question I repeatedly ask myself.

VERLAINE: No doubt you regarded it as another stage in your private Odyssey. Only by plunging ever deeper, if I may mix my myths, will you attain the right to graze on the upper slopes of Parnassus.

RIMBAUD: Your attack is unusually coherent this morning.

VERLAINE: My theory differs from yours. My theory is that you are like Musset.

RIMBAUD: What?

VERLAINE: Rather a provocative comparison, don't you think, in view of your continual attacks on the wretched man?

RIMBAUD: Explain it.

VERLAINE: Well, I simply mean that like Musset or one of Musset's heroes, you tried on the cloak of vice, and now it's stuck to your skin. You came back here with me because you wanted to, and because you needed to.

RIMBAUD: Well now, that's quite original for you, even though you have made your customary mistake.

VERLAINE: What's that?

RIMBAUD: Getting carried away by an idea because it's aesthetically plausible rather than actually true.

VERLAINE: Oh, there are less subtle reasons for your putting up with me.

RIMBAUD: Such as?

VERLAINE: Such as the fact that I support you.

(*Silence.*)

RIMBAUD: Your mind is almost as ugly as your body.

(*Silence. They look at each other.* VERLAINE *struggles with himself for a moment, then, suddenly, his face goes blank and he strides across the stage.*)

RIMBAUD (*uneasily*): Where are you going?

VERLAINE: To the kitchen. It's lunchtime.

(*Exit* VERLAINE. RIMBAUD *pours himself a drink rather shakily, and swallows it. He seems puzzled. A moment later,* VERLAINE *enters again, carrying in one hand, a herring, and in the other, a bottle of oil.* RIMBAUD *looks at him, then bursts out laughing.* VERLAINE *scarcely responds.*)

RIMBAUD: God, you look such a cunt.

(VERLAINE *doesn't answer. Instead, he puts the herring and the bottle of oil down on the table, and strides across the stage, away from the kitchen.*)

Where are you going?

(*Exit* VERLAINE.)

Where are you going? (*He looks frightened and vulnerable.*)

CURTAIN

SCENE THREE

A room in the Hôtel de Courtrai, Brussels; 10th July, 1873.
RIMBAUD *is packing. He looks tired and rather sad. The door bursts open and* VERLAINE *enters. He is drunk, which in his case means over-excitement and a certain belligerence, rather than incoherence or physical unsteadiness.*

RIMBAUD: Where have you been?

VERLAINE: Out. I went, I went to the Spanish Embassy again, to see if they would change their minds. But they wouldn't, it's ridiculous, it's bloody ridiculous. I'm willing to fight, I

said, and die for your cause, you can't afford to turn away
volunteers. But they said they weren't taking on any
foreigners. Then, I said, you deserve to lose the bloody war,
and I hope you do.

RIMBAUD: And were you at the Spanish Embassy all morning?

VERLAINE: No.

RIMBAUD: You're drunk.

VERLAINE: I have yes had a few drinks.

(*Silence.* VERLAINE *notices that* RIMBAUD *is packing.*)
What are you doing?

RIMBAUD: I'm packing.

VERLAINE: Where are you going?

RIMBAUD: I've told you already, I'm going back to Paris. And if
you'll kindly give me some money for the fare, I shall leave
this evening.

VERLAINE: No, listen, listen, we're going back to London.

RIMBAUD: We are not going back to London.

VERLAINE: Yes, look, I've been thinking it over this morning, it's
by far the best idea.

RIMBAUD: Then why did you go to the Spanish Embassy?

VERLAINE: I didn't.

(*Silence.*)

RIMBAUD: I am going back to Paris.

VERLAINE: It won't happen again, look, I'll never walk out on
you again like that, I promise.

RIMBAUD: No you won't, I'm not giving you the chance. What
did you expect me to do on my own in London with no
money? Mm? I ran along the quayside shouting for you
not to leave me and you just turned your back on me.

VERLAINE: What was I supposed to do, jump overboard?

RIMBAUD: Now you want me to forgive and forget.

VERLAINE: I was very hurt.

RIMBAUD: I can't think why. God knows, I've said far worse
things to you than that. Anyway you really did look a cunt.

(VERLAINE *bridles, then controls himself.*)

VERLAINE: Don't go. Just wait another day or two and think it
over.

RIMBAUD: I've thought it over.

VERLAINE: Or else, what about this, I had another idea this morning. I thought I might go to Paris.

RIMBAUD: What?

VERLAINE: I thought I might go to Paris and try to find Mathilde.

RIMBAUD (*after considering this*): Well, all right, I don't mind travelling with you.

VERLAINE: No, no, you would stay here in Brussels.

RIMBAUD: Are you mad?

VERLAINE: No, don't you see, it would be absolutely fatal if you came back with me. She'd never take me back.

RIMBAUD: I doubt she will anyway.

VERLAINE: Well then, I'll come back to Brussels, and we can go back to London.

RIMBAUD: You're out of your mind.

VERLAINE: Do you realize what day it is tomorrow?

RIMBAUD: Friday.

VERLAINE: It's my anniversary, it's our third anniversary. And I haven't seen her, my wife, for almost a year. A year ago, here in Brussels, we made love, and I haven't seen her since. And I haven't seen my son for more than a year. She won't answer my letters. Do you know that I wrote to her last week, and told her if she didn't come to Brussels within three days, I'd commit suicide? And she didn't even answer.

RIMBAUD: Ah, but then you didn't commit suicide.

VERLAINE: I suppose you think that's funny.

RIMBAUD: No, it's pitiful. How many people did you write and tell you were going to commit suicide? I'm surprised you didn't send out invitations.

VERLAINE: How can you be so callous?

RIMBAUD: Callous? You abandon me in London and then summon me to Brussels and expect me to hang about while you decide whether you're going to go back to your wife, join the army, or shoot yourself. Then, when you fail to achieve any of these aims, as you undoubtedly will, we'll to go back to London again.

I'm not going to. It's all over. I'm leaving you.

120

VERLAINE: You can't. You can't. (*Paces up and down for a moment.*) Where's mother?

RIMBAUD: Next door, I suppose, in her room. I asked her to let me have some money, but she wouldn't give it to me until you came back. I'll go and ask her again.

VERLAINE: No, no, wait a minute. Look, I'll give you the money. I just want to talk to you a minute. (*He paces up and down, smiles nervously at* RIMBAUD.) Hot, isn't it?

I think we can start again. I don't think it would be too difficult to go back to the beginning. I know it's my fault, all the trouble we've had recently, but it's only because of Mathilde, because I still loved Mathilde. It's finished with her now, I know I shall never see her again. Look, it's summer. Don't you remember last summer, when we set out, how wonderful it was. I remember evenings. . . . There's no need to go back to London if you don't want to. We could go south. Late summer on the Mediterranean, we could live more cheaply there, we wouldn't need to work, we could dedicate ourselves to warmth. Or Africa, we could go to North Africa, I know you've always wanted to go to Africa. Just for a month and then make up your mind.

Look at the sun.

(*Long silence.*)

RIMBAUD: No.

VERLAINE: Why not?

RIMBAUD (*gently*): I can't. It's no good. It's too late.

VERLAINE: No, it's not. I promise you it's not. You know if you leave me, you'll kill me. I can't bear to be alone. I don't exist without someone else. I don't care if you stay with me out of pity, as long as you stay.

RIMBAUD: I can't.

VERLAINE: Why not? What more can I say to make you stay? Don't you care? Have you no idea of what this means to me?

RIMBAUD: Oh, for God's sake, stop whining.

(*Silence.* VERLAINE *goes over to look out of the window. He mops his brow with a handkerchief.*)

VERLAINE: It's very hot.

RIMBAUD: I should take your coat off.

VERLAINE: I will. (*He slips his coat off, walks over to the door, and hangs it up.*) I did some shopping this morning. (*He takes something out of his pocket, and turns towards* RIMBAUD.) I bought a gun. (*He points a revolver at* RIMBAUD.)

RIMBAUD: What for?

VERLAINE: For you. And for me. For everybody.

RIMBAUD: I hope you bought plenty of ammunition.

(VERLAINE *moves a chair in front of the door, and sits astride it, pointing the revolver at* RIMBAUD *over the back of the chair.* RIMBAUD *leans against the opposite wall, smiling.*)

VERLAINE: I'm not going to let you go, you know.

RIMBAUD: Well, this is rather an entertaining number. We haven't seen this one before.

VERLAINE (*cries out*): I'll kill you!

RIMBAUD: Oh, pull yourself together.

(*Silence.*)

VERLAINE: Have you forgotten what you said in your letter?

RIMBAUD: What letter?

VERLAINE: The letter you wrote me last week, the day after I left you.

RIMBAUD: It's of no relevance.

VERLAINE: Oh, yes it is. You apologized. You begged me to come back. You said it was all your fault. You said you loved me. You said it would be all right in the future. You said you were crying as you wrote. I could see your tears on the paper.

RIMBAUD: Well, I didn't have any money, did I? That was before I thought of pawning your clothes.

(VERLAINE *springs to his feet, shaking with rage. He raises the revolver and fires at* RIMBAUD, *then, apparently stunned at the noise of the retort, fires again into the floor.* RIMBAUD *is clutching at his left wrist, and staring at it in amazement and horror, as the blood pours down over his hand. He shies away, as* VERLAINE *moves towards him.*)

VERLAINE: Oh, God, I'm sorry, I didn't mean to.

RIMBAUD: Look what you've done.

VERLAINE: I'm sorry, I didn't mean to.

RIMBAUD: Look.

(VERLAINE *bursts into tears. He tries to give* RIMBAUD *the revolver.*)

VELAINE: Oh, for God's sake, kill me, kill me, shoot me.

RIMBAUD: What?

VERLAINE: Shoot me.

RIMBAUD: How can I, you silly bugger, you've just blown a hole in my hand.

(*A furious banging at the door and a female voice shouting:* 'Paul, Paul'. . . . VERLAINE *drops the revolver.* RIMBAUD *begins to laugh hysterically.*)

VERLAINE: Oh God, what have I done?

RIMBAUD: You missed.

(*Blackout.*)

CURTAIN

SCENE FOUR

Brussels, 10th–19th July, 1873.

This scene is constructed from fragments of VERLAINE's *trial. On one side of the stage,* RIMBAUD *lies in bed, his arm in a sling.* VERLAINE *sits on the other side of the stage, in court. The magistrate,* JUDGE THÉODORE T'SERSTEVENS, *and his* CLERK *commute from one side of the stage to the other. When the scene opens, the* CLERK *is taking down* RIMBAUD's *statement.*

RIMBAUD: . . . When the wound had been dressed, the three of us returned to the hotel. Verlaine asked me continually not to leave him and to stay with him; but I refused to agree and left the hotel about seven o'clock in the evening, accompanied by Verlaine and his mother. Not far from the Place Rouppe, Verlaine went on a few paces ahead, and then turned towards me: I saw him put his hand in his pocket to get his revolver, so I turned and walked away. I

123

met a police officer and told him what had happened to
me, and he invited Verlaine to accompany him to the police
station.

 If Verlaine had let me leave freely, I would have taken
no action against him for the wound he inflicted on
me. . . .

VERLAINE: . . . I swear to tell the whole truth and nothing but
 the truth, so help me God and all His saints.

JUDGE: Have you any previous convictions?

VERLAINE: No.

JUDGE: What is the motive behind your presence in Brussels?

VERLAINE: I was hoping that my wife might come and join me
 here, as she had already done so on one occasion since our
 separation.

JUDGE: I fail to see how the departure of a friend could have
 cast you into such despair. Did there not exist between you
 and Rimbaud other relations besides those of friendship?

VERLAINE: No; this is a suggestion slanderously invented by my
 wife and her family to harm me; I have been accused of
 this in my wife's petition for divorce.

JUDGE: Both doctors have testified that on the basis of their
 examination they are satisfied that you have recently
 indulged in both active and passive sodomy.

VERLAINE: Yes.

JUDGE: Then do you deny that you are a practising sodomist?

VERLAINE: The word is sodomite. . . .

 (*Pause. The* JUDGE *and the* CLERK *return to the court, where
 the* CLERK *reads* RIMBAUD's *final statement, as the lights dim.*)

CLERK: . . . I, the undersigned, Arthur Rimbaud,
 declare it to be the truth that on Thursday, the
 10th inst., at the moment when M. Paul Verlaine fired at
 me and wounded me slightly in the left wrist, M. Verlaine
 was in such a complete state of drunkenness, that he had no
 idea of what he was doing.

 I am utterly convinced that there was no criminal
premeditation in his action;

I further declare that I am willing to withdraw from any criminal, correctional or civil action against him, and as from today renounce the benefits of any proceedings which may be brought against M. Verlaine by the Public Prosecutor arising from this matter. . . .

JUDGE: . . . The accused, Paul-Marie Verlaine, is committed for trial at the criminal court, charged under article 399 of the Penal Code, of grievous bodily harm. The preliminary examination is closed. . . .

CLERK (*in the darkness*): Paul-Marie Verlaine, the court finds you guilty of grievous bodily harm and sentences you to a fine of 200 francs and 2 years' imprisonment.

CURTAIN

SCENE FIVE

The Black Forest, near Stuttgart; 28th February, 1875.
The curtain goes up on an empty stage. The scene suggests a clearing in a wood by a river. Sounds of laughter offstage. Presently RIMBAUD *enters, a little better dressed than in previous scenes. It is evening. Moonlight.*

RIMBAUD: This way.
    (*He laughs.* VERLAINE *enters.*)
    When was this, anyway?
VERLAINE: Earlier this month.
    (RIMBAUD *laughs again.*)
RIMBAUD: And they threw you out?
VERLAINE: Certainly not. After a week the Father Superior and I agreed that it wasn't really the life for me.
RIMBAUD: This'll do. (*He squats down on the ground and lights his clay pipe.*) And what led you to believe that you were cut

out to be a Trappist monk?

VERLAINE: I don't know. Perhaps it was nostalgia for prison. It was terrible coming out, you know. I'd got used to the quiet and the routine, they treated me very well, and I was sober and able to do a lot of good work. Then, when I came out and couldn't even get to see Mathilde's lawyer, let alone Mathilde, I thought the best thing to do might be to . . . withdraw. To a monastery, to live a quiet, simple life with God.

RIMBAUD: But it turned out to be a teetotal order.

VERLAINE: I told you I got used to being sober in prison.

RIMBAUD: I'm pleased to see the situation is not wholly irreversible.

VERLAINE: Well, tonight is different. Tonight is a celebration. It's really . . . wonderful to see you again. (*Pause.*) After all this time. (*Pause.*) I hope you never thought . . . that I was angry with you.

RIMBAUD: No.

VERLAINE: I mean, I know you had no idea that I might get put away for so long, I certainly . . . forgave you for it.

RIMBAUD: Did you?

VERLAINE: Oh, yes.

RIMBAUD: I didn't forgive you.

VERLAINE: What for?

RIMBAUD: For missing.

(VERLAINE *laughs uneasily. Silence.*)

VERLAINE: It's very pleasant here.

RIMBAUD: Im Schwarzwald.

VERLAINE: How is your German?

RIMBAUD: Flourishing.

(*Silence.*)

VERLAINE: Not very warm, is it?

RIMBAUD: Why did you come here?

VERLAINE: What?

RIMBAUD: I want to know your reason for coming here.

VERLAINE: Well . . . to see you, of course. I wanted to talk to you, to discuss certain things with you.

RIMBAUD: You want us to love each other in Jesus, am I right?

126

VERLAINE: Well. . . .

RIMBAUD: All right, I'm listening, tell me about it.

VERLAINE: It's very difficult to talk seriously if you're going to be so aggressive. I've changed, you know.

RIMBAUD: Go on, talk seriously, never mind what I say. A missionary should be prepared to meet aggression from the unenlightened. Tell me about your conversion. Was it a bit of an occasion? Was there a celestial voice?

VERLAINE: Recently it occurred to me that your anger and disgust prove how ready you are for conversion. And anyway I often think you do believe in God. Even in the old days, when you used to paint up "Sod God" in the urinals in Paris, you must have had some faith. You can't blaspheme if you don't believe.

RIMBAUD: No, you're wrong. You couldn't blaspheme if nobody believed. Your own feelings have nothing to do with it.

VERLAINE: I just want you to follow my example. The day of my conversion was one of the happiest of my life. It was the day the governor came and told me Mathilde had been granted a legal separation. I lay down and looked at my life, and there was nothing, nothing. It seemed to me the only thing I could do was submit myself to God, and ask Him to forgive me, and help me to face my situation. And He did. I promise you He did.

RIMBAUD (*kindly*): Don't let's talk about it any more.

VERLAINE: Why not?

RIMBAUD: It's dangerous.

VERLAINE: But I want you to find some direction to your life. I want God to help you to achieve your aims.

RIMBAUD: Aims? I have no aims.

VERLAINE: Well, I mean your writing.

RIMBAUD: I've stopped writing.

VERLAINE: What?

RIMBAUD: I have stopped writing.

VERLAINE: I don't understand. . . .

RIMBAUD: Well, let me put it another way: I no longer write.

VERLAINE: Yes, but why not?

RIMBAUD: Because I have nothing more to say. If I ever had

127

anything to say in the first place.

VERLAINE: How can you say that?

(RIMBAUD *laughs at* VERLAINE's *unhappy choice of words*.)
How can you?

RIMBAUD: Well, as you know, I started life as a self-appointed visionary, and creator of a new literature. But as time wore on, and it took me longer and longer to write less and less, and I looked back at some of the absurdities of my earlier work, at some of the things I thought were so good when I wrote them, I saw it was pointless to go on. The world is too old, there's nothing new, it's all been said. Anything that can be put into words is not worth putting into words.

VERLAINE: The truth is always worth putting into words.

RIMBAUD: The truth is too limited to be interesting.

VERLAINE: What do you mean?—Truth is infinite.

RIMBAUD: If you're referring to the truth that was revealed to you in prison by an angel of the Lord, you may be wrong. After all, what makes you think it's any truer than the rather different views you asserted with equal confidence three years ago?

VERLAINE: Well, obviously one develops.

RIMBAUD: And have you developed?

VERLAINE: Yes.

(*Long silence*.)

RIMBAUD: Then, here in the wilderness, I offer you an archetypal choice—the choice between my body and my soul.

VERLAINE: What?

(*Long silence*.)

RIMBAUD: Choose.

VERLAINE: Your body.

(*Silence*.)

RIMBAUD: See, the ninety-eight wounds of Our Saviour burst and bleed.

VERLAINE: Please.

RIMBAUD: So you didn't come here to convert me.

VERLAINE: No.

RIMBAUD: And the iron glove conceals a velvet hand.

(VERLAINE *moves towards* RIMBAUD, *touches his shoulder*.)

Don't.

(*Silence.*)

So God turned out to be a poor substitute for Mathilde and me, suffering, as he does, from certain tangible disadvantages.

VERLAINE: Surely my sins are a matter for my own conscience.

RIMBAUD: They would be if you had one.

VERLAINE: Anyway, why should it worry you?

RIMBAUD: Because I hate your miserable weakness.

VERLAINE: Is overcoming my conscience weakness? Or strength?

RIMBAUD: Don't be absurd.

(*Silence.*)

VERLAINE: But I see no clash between loving God and loving you.

RIMBAUD: Come on, let's go back.

VERLAINE: No, listen, I sat in my cell and thought how much love I had in me, and how happy we could be, it should be easy, it should be the easiest thing in the world, why isn't it?

RIMBAUD: It never worked with us. And it will never work for either of us.

VERLAINE: Of course it will. Why should you think that? Why are you so destructive?

RIMBAUD: Probably because I no longer have any sympathy for you.

VERLAINE: Don't you feel anything for me?

RIMBAUD: Only a kind of mild contempt.

VERLAINE: But how can you change like that? How is it possible?

RIMBAUD: I don't know.

VERLAINE: I wanted us to go away together.

RIMBAUD: Yes.

VERLAINE: What are you going to do?

RIMBAUD: I'm going to finish learning German. And then I'm going to leave Europe. Alone.

VERLAINE: What about me?

RIMBAUD: You'll have to go away and find somebody else.

VERLAINE: I can't. Please. (*He puts his arms round* RIMBAUD.) Please.

RIMBAUD: Let me go.

> (VERLAINE *clings on to him.* RIMBAUD *speaks, as he has done throughout this last exchange, with great weariness.*)
>
> Let go.

VERLAINE: Please.

> (RIMBAUD *hits* VERLAINE *hard, stunning him. He hits him again, carefully and methodically, until he collapses in an untidy heap.* RIMBAUD *straightens him out almost tenderly, then stands looking down at him for a moment.*)

RIMBAUD (*quietly*): Good-bye. (*He exits.*)

CURTAIN

SCENE SIX

A café in Paris; 29th February, 1892.

It is early evening and the rather squalid café, is not very full. Presently VERLAINE *enters. He is now 47, but looks much older, a derelict carnal hulk. His clothes are correct, much as they were in the first scene of the play, but worn shabby. He has a walking-stick, and limps heavily, dragging his left leg behind him. He is accompanied by* EUGÉNIE KRANTZ, *who is about fifty and a semi-retired prostitute. Her accent sounds like a crude parody of* RIMBAUD's.

VERLAINE: Evening.

> (*A few muttered replies. He and* EUGÉNIE *sit at one of the tables.*)
>
> Absinthe, please. Two.
>
> (*The* BARMAN *nods, pours drinks behind the bar.*)
>
> God, I'm tired.

EUGÉNIE (*sniggers*): Not surprised.

VERLAINE: You're beautiful, Eugénie.

EUGÉNIE: I know. (*She laughs raucously.*)

VERLAINE: Don't let anyone tell you different. If I think you're beautiful, then you're beautiful.

> (*The* BARMAN *brings the drinks.*)

130

BARMAN: Someone been in to see you this afternoon, M. Verlaine.

VERLAINE: Who?

BARMAN: A young lady. She didn't leave her name.

VERLAINE: A young lady?

BARMAN: Well, in her thirties, I suppose. She seemed very keen to see you, so I said you'd be sure to be in later, and she said she'd come back. She said it was quite important.

VERLAINE: Thanks.

(*The* BARMAN *turns away.*)

Just a minute. . . . What did she look like?

BARMAN: Oh, not bad, monsieur, not bad.

VERLAINE: Thanks.

(*Silence.*)

EUGÉNIE: Who is it?

VERLAINE: What?

EUGÉNIE: Who is it?

VERLAINE: How should I know?

EUGÉNIE: It can't be Esther, it's too young for her. So it must be someone else.

VERLAINE: I told you I haven't seen Esther since I came out of hospital.

EUGÉNIE: You told me! Who is it?

VERLAINE: I don't know.

(*Silence.*)

It must be some business matter.

EUGÉNIE: Business, eh?

VERLAINE: Yes. I'd appreciate it if you'd let me talk to her alone when she comes.

EUGÉNIE: Oh, charming, that is. Lovely. I'm supposed to go and sit on my own, am I, while you talk to your new girl-friends?

VERLAINE: I promise you, I don't know who it is, and if it's a business matter, I'd rather talk to her alone.

EUGÉNIE (*a threat*): I shall go and talk to that gentleman over there.

VERLAINE: Well, you must do as you like.

EUGÉNIE: Perhaps he'll turn out a bit more respectful than you are.

(*Silence.*)

VERLAINE: Two more, please.

(*The* BARMAN *comes over, and pours the drinks.*)

Can you let me have some money, please?

EUGÉNIE: Eh?

VERLAINE: I haven't any money on me.

EUGÉNIE: Well, don't ask me for money.

VERLAINE: Look, Eugénie, I'm not feeling very well, and I don't want to argue with you. Now will you kindly give me some money.

EUGÉNIE: You haven't done any work today.

VERLAINE: I haven't been feeling very well.

EUGÉNIE: Well, if you don't do any work, you can't expect to be paid.

VERLAINE: Look, it's my money.

EUGÉNIE: It wouldn't be much longer if I let you get your hands on it.

VERLAINE: I just want a few. . . .

EUGÉNIE: No.

(ISABELLE RIMBAUD *enters. She is 31, very respectfully dressed in mourning, and already something of an old maid. There is some resemblance between her and her brother, but this is most noticeable when she speaks—with* RIMBAUD's *soft, provincial accent. She goes over and has a word with the* BARMAN, *who points out* VERLAINE *to her. He is still arguing with* EUGÉNIE *in a violent undertone.*)

VERLAINE: Now, listen, Eugénie, if you don't give me some money at once, there'll be trouble, do you understand?

EUGÉNIE: I haven't got any money with me. So you'll have to do without, won't you?

VERLAINE: You're making me very angry.

EUGÉNIE: Anyway, here comes your girl-friend, by the look of it. So I'll be leaving you. (*She gets up, then leans forward and speaks in a venomous whisper.*) And if you don't come back tonight, you'll find your things in the street.

(*She leaves him, and while he is speaking to* ISABELLE, *she joins one of the men sitting at a table at the back of the stage.* VERLAINE *rises, turns to meet* ISABELLE.)

ISABELLE (*tentatively*): M. Verlaine?

VERLAINE: At your service, mademoiselle.

ISABELLE: I am Isabelle Rimbaud.

VERLAINE: Pardon? (*He sinks into his chair.*)

ISABELLE: I am Isabelle Rimbaud. I am M. Arthur Rimbaud's sister.

VERLAINE: Of course, er, of course, please sit down, mademoiselle. You must excuse me for being so rude, but I find it difficult to stand.

(ISABELLE *sits.*)

I heard, we heard the tragic news a couple of months ago. I could hardly believe it, he was so young. And then, he'd been reported dead before, you know, earlier. I was deeply . . . affected by his death, although I hadn't seen him for so long.

ISABELLE: I didn't know whether you'd heard.

VERLAINE: Is it true . . . is it true he had to have his leg amputated?

ISABELLE: Yes.

(*Silence.*)

I'll get straight to the point, M. Verlaine, I don't have very much time.

VERLAINE: You look a bit like him, you know. Your eyes . . . are not unlike his.

ISABELLE: So I've been told.

VERLAINE: Would you like a drink?

ISABELLE: No thank you very much. It's really a business matter I want to discuss with you. M. Vanier said you might be able to help me.

VERLAINE: Well, I'll do what I can.

ISABELLE: On the day my brother died, a volume of his poems was published in Paris, wasn't it?

VERLAINE: You mean *The Reliquary*?

ISABELLE: That's right. The publication was completely un-authorized, and there was an anonymous preface full of the most outrageous and libellous statements, which claimed to be a biography of my brother. My mother and I were very upset by it.

133

VERLAINE: Yes, well, er, I believe M. Genonceaux is the man
    you should see about this. He's the editor.

ISABELLE: I know. I haven't been able to get hold of M.
    Genonceaux.

VERLAINE: Anyway, the book's now been withdrawn from
    circulation.

ISABELLE: I know. But my mother and I are anxious to prevent
    anything like this from happening again. And M. Vanier
    said you might be able to help us.

VERLAINE: I? How?

ISABELLE: Well, I understand you have a large number of my
    brother's manuscripts.

VERLAINE: I have . . . some, yes.

ISABELLE: My mother and I would be very grateful if you'd
    return them.
    (*Silence.*)

VERLAINE: I've always . . . used the utmost discretion in every-
    thing concerning your brother. I think I can say that I've
    always defended his interests. Since his name began to be
    well known, various newspapers and magazines have
    printed forgeries, you know, and I've made myself
    responsible for putting a stop to it and making sure that
    everything that comes out under his name is his work. I'm
    quite fanatical about it, it's very important to me. We did
    our best work when we were together, you know, both of
    us. Since then, as far as I'm concerned, it's all been just
    one long footnote.

ISABELLE: I didn't know his name was all that well known.

VERLAINE: Oh, yes.

ISABELLE: That makes it even more vital that we collect up all
    his manuscripts. Perhaps I should explain our intentions to
    you. Did you know he was converted before he died?

VERLAINE: Converted?

ISABELLE: Yes. I reasoned with him and prayed for him for
    weeks while he was ill and about a fortnight before he died,
    he asked to be confessed. After that, we prayed together
    every day, and the chaplain said that he had never
    encountered faith as strong as Arthur's. Do you know, in

spite of the tragic circumstances, the day Arthur asked for the chaplain was one of the happiest of my life.

VERLAINE: So he took the last Sacraments?

ISABELLE: No, unfortunately they weren't able to give him communion, because he couldn't keep anything down, and they were afraid there might be an involuntary sacrilege. But I know his soul was saved.

VERLAINE (*without irony*): That must be a great comfort.

ISABELLE: Yes. Anyway, you'll appreciate now how important it is for my mother and I to get hold of his writings.

VERLAINE: Er . . . ?

ISABELLE: The point is, M. Verlaine, to speak frankly, a number of the poems he wrote in extreme youth were rather . . . indecent, and in some cases even profane. He would never have wished to be remembered for them. My mother and I plan to as it were separate the wheat from the tares, and destroy those of his works which we feel he would have destroyed himself.

VERLAINE: I see.

ISABELLE: We were amazed, in fact, that the poems in *The Reliquary* were thought to be worthy of publication. We supposed that they could only have been published for motives of profit. I'd be very interested to know who pocketed the author's royalties.

VERLAINE (*guiltily*): Yes . . . well, er, I couldn't tell you.

ISABELLE: Here's my mother's card. Perhaps you could send the manuscripts to this address.

VERLAINE: As a matter of fact, Vanier and I were planning an edition of Rimbaud's complete works.

ISABELLE: Yes, M. Vanier told me.

VERLAINE: Well, don't you think that there's . . . a place for the works you mentioned in our edition? I mean, surely his conversion becomes even more striking if it's seen against . . . some of the things he wrote when he was young.

ISABELLE: I'm sure these considerations will be borne in mind.

VERLAINE: Yes, yes, of course. . . .

ISABELLE: I wonder if you could give us your address, so that I can get in touch with you if it's necessary.

VERLAINE: Well, I . . . don't really have an address, mademoiselle. I spend a lot of time in hospital, you see, and my address seems to . . . change quite often.

ISABELLE: I see. Well, I think that's about all, M. Verlaine.

VERLAINE: It occurs to me, that if you want Rimbaud's manuscripts, my wife might be able to help you.

ISABELLE: Your wife?

VERLAINE: Yes. I still think of her as my wife, although I'm told she's taken advantage of the Gospel according to the Civil Service, and married someone else. I haven't seen her since before . . . for about twenty years. I spent years trying to get her to send me Rimbaud's manuscripts and letters.

ISABELLE: Yes. Thank you.

VERLAINE: She's a spiteful and wicked woman. Do you know that my son will be twenty-one this year, and I haven't seen him since he was eight?

ISABELLE: I think I should be going, M. Verlaine, I'd like to get back to my hotel before it gets dark.

VERLAINE: Wait. Please. Just a minute. I wonder if you could, before you go, just tell me something about . . . your brother. You see, the last time I saw him, in Stuttgart, must have been about seventeen years ago, when he was over there learning German. After that, the reports were so vague. We heard he was in Abyssinia, we heard he was dead, and later that he was alive, and all kinds of rumours. I wonder if you could just . . . fill in the details a little, that's all.

ISABELLE: I don't know that there's very much to tell. He travelled. He was a building consultant in Cyprus for some time, then he moved on to Aden and got a job with a trading firm. He established a new depot for them in Abyssinia about five years ago, which he managed and ran himself.

VERLAINE: But how did he die?

ISABELLE: He had a tumour on his knee.

VERLAINE: That's very strange.

ISABELLE: Why?

VERLAINE: Because that's what I have, a . . . tumour on my

knee.

ISABELLE: It would have been all right if he'd done something about it sooner, if he hadn't been so conscientious about his work. There was no doctor there, but he insisted on staying until the pain became unbearable. After that, it took him two months to get back to Marseilles, and they amputated his leg—but by that time it was too late to do anything for him.

VERLAINE: How terrible.

ISABELLE: In fact, after the operation it was worse. They tried to fit him with a wooden leg, but he couldn't manage it. They'd had to amputate too high and the stump couldn't take the weight. He said, after the operation, he kept saying, that if he'd known what it was going to be like, he'd never have let them amputate. He hated the hospital so much, that at the end of July he left and came home.

VERLAINE: Was he alone in Marseilles?

ISABELLE: Oh yes. Mother went down for the operation, but she couldn't afford to stay with him, because it was getting near to harvest-time.

(*A burst of raucous laughter from* EUGÉNIE.)

ISABELLE: When he got home things weren't too bad at first, but before long he lost the use of his right arm, and the pain spread and increased. The doctor gave him drugs to stop the pain, and he became delirious. I remember one night, I was woken up by a terrible crash from his room. I rushed up there and found my brother lying face down on the floor, naked. He told me he had opened his eyes and it was dawn, and time to go, to lead his caravan of ivory and musk to the coast. He said, he kept saying, that he wanted to go back to the sun, and that the sun would heal him, and eventually he left for Marseilles and I went with him. He intended to travel on from there to Aden, but when he got there he was too ill, and he went back into hospital. The paralysis gradually spread, and a large tumour appeared on the inside of his stump. I think God kept him alive long enough to repent, so that he could be saved.

VERLAINE: Yes. The last time we met, in Stuttgart, we spoke of religion. I had just been converted, and I tried very hard to convince him of the truth. Perhaps I helped him in some small way.

(*Silence.* EUGÉNIE *exits on the arm of the man she has been talking to.*)

VERLAINE: Did he . . . I don't suppose he ever mentioned me.

ISABELLE: No.

VERLAINE: It was a long time ago.

ISABELLE: It's getting dark. I must go.

VERLAINE: But still. . . .

(ISABELLE *stands up, and* VERLAINE, *at first startled by her movement, drags himself painfully to his feet.*)

ISABELLE: Good-bye, M. Verlaine.

(*They shake hands.*)

VERLAINE: Won't you let me see you to your hotel?

ISABELLE: No, it's quite all right.

VERLAINE: Are you sure?

ISABELLE (*formally*): It was an honour to meet such a distinguished poet.

VERLAINE: It was a great pleasure to meet you, mademoiselle.

ISABELLE: You have mother's card there, don't you? Don't forget to send us Arthur's manuscripts.

VERLAINE: No.

ISABELLE: Good-bye, monsieur.

VERLAINE: Good night.

(*Exit* ISABELLE. VERLAINE *sits down. For a moment there is absolute silence. Then he tears up* MME RIMBAUD's *visiting card, smiling a little to himself.*)

Eugénie? Where are you?

Absinthe. Two, please.

(*The* BARMAN *pours two absinthes into the two glasses already on the table.* VERLAINE *drinks.*)

It was a long time ago. But I remember the first time I saw him. That evening in the Mautés' main room. When we walked in, he was standing with his back to us, looking out of the window. He turned round and spoke, and then I saw him, and I was amazed how beautiful he was. He was sixteen.

Since he died I see him every night. My great and radiant sin.

(RIMBAUD *enters, dressed as he was in the first scene, but moving with more confidence, smiling, handsome, lithe. He sits down at the table next to* VERLAINE *and they smile at each other*.)

Tell me if you love me.

RIMBAUD: You know I'm very fond of you. We've been very happy sometimes.

(*Silence*.)

Do you love me?

VERLAINE: Yes.

RIMBAUD: Then put your hands on the table.

VERLAINE: What?

RIMBAUD: Put your hands on the table.

(VERLAINE *does so*.)

Palm upwards.

(VERLAINE *turns his hands palm upwards*. RIMBAUD *looks at them for a moment, and then bends forward and kisses them. Then he gets up, smiles at* VERLAINE, *and exits. There is a long silence*.)

VERLAINE: We were always happy. Always. I remember.

(VERLAINE *sits alone in a pool of light, which gradually dims as he speaks*.)

Eugénie?

What I love in old, sad flesh is the youth which whispers around it. I love its memories of youth.

I remember our first summer, how happy it was, the happiest time of my life. Wandering across Belgium, eating turnips and huddling in ditches. He's not dead, he's trapped and living inside me. As long as I live, he has some kind of flickering and limited life. It's always the same words and the same gestures—the same images: I walk behind him across a steep ploughed field; I sit, talking to him in a darkening room, until I can barely see his profile and his expressive hand; I lie in bed at dawn and watch him sleeping and see how nervously his hand brushes at his cheek. I remember him of an evening and he lives.

Absinthe.
Are you there? Eugénie? Are you there?
(*Darkness.*)

CURTAIN

APPENDIX

Extract from one of Rimbaud's last letters to his sister:

Marseilles, 15th July, 1891

My dear Isabelle,

... I spend day and night torturing myself, trying to think of ways to get about. I want to do all kinds of things, live, get away from here: but it's impossible, at least, it'll be impossible for months, if not for ever. All I can think about are these damn crutches: without them, I can't take a step, I can't exist. I can't even get dressed without the most terrible gymnastics. It's true I can run now with my crutches; but I can't go up or down stairs, and if the ground isn't level, shifting the strain from one shoulder to the other is very tiring. I still have very painful neuralgia in my right arm and shoulder, and in addition to this, the crutches cut into my armpits. My left leg is very painful as well—and the worst thing is having to behave like an acrobat all day to have any sort of existence at all.

My dear sister, I've been thinking about what really caused my illness. The climate in Harar is cold from November to March. I never used to wear many clothes—just a pair of canvas trousers and a cotton shirt. Also I quite often used to walk 15 to 40 kilometres a day, leading lunatic processions across steep, mountainous country. I think I must have developed some arthritic trouble caused by fatigue and the heat and the cold. It all started with a kind of hammer blow which used to strike me under the kneecap every so often. The joint was very dry and my thigh was stiff. The next thing was the veins all round the knee swelled up, which made me think they were varicose. I kept on going for walks, and working harder than ever, I thought it was just a chill. Then the pain inside my knee got worse, every step I took, it was like a nail being driven in. I was still walking, but it got more and more difficult; so I used to ride, and whenever I dismounted, I felt completely crippled. Then the back of my knee swelled up, my knee-

141

cap got very fleshy, so did my shin. The blood wasn't circulating properly, and my nerves throbbed from my ankle right the way up to my back. I couldn't walk without a heavy limp, and it was getting worse and worse. But I still had a lot of essential work to do. I started bandaging the whole of my leg, massaging it, bathing it, and so on, but it was no good. I lost my appetite. I was suffering from stubborn insomnia. I got weaker and lost a lot of weight. About the 15th March, I decided to stay in bed between my desk and papers and the window, so that I could keep an eye on the scales at the end of the yard, and I paid people to keep the business going, while I lay there with my leg stretched out. Every day the knee swelled up more until it was like a large ball. I noticed that the back of the shin bone was much bigger at the top than on the other leg. I couldn't move the kneecap, it was soaked in the muck which formed the swelling, which, I was horrified to see, turned as hard as bone within a few days. A week later, my whole leg was stiff, I couldn't bend it at all; I had to drag myself along the ground to the latrines. In the meantime my calf and my thigh got thinner and thinner, while the knee joint swelled, hardened, and seemed to turn into bone; and my physical and mental weakness increased. At the end of March, I decided to leave. I sold up everything in a few days—at a loss; and as the stiffness and pain prevented me from riding a mule or even a camel, I had a litter made with a curtain roof, and hired 16 men, who took a fortnight to get me to Zeyla. On the second day of the journey, we went on far ahead of the caravan, and were caught in a rainstorm in the middle of the desert. I lay for 16 hours in the pouring rain, with no shelter and no possibility of movement; this did me a great deal of harm. On the way I was never able to get out of the litter. They set up the tent above me wherever they'd happened to put me down. I used to dig a hole with my hands near the edge of the litter, crawl over to it with great difficulty, relieve myself into it, and then fill it with earth again. In the morning they'd take the tent away, then they'd take me away. I arrived at Zeyla exhausted and paralysed. I had only four hours' rest before the steamer left for Aden. They bundled me on to the bridge on my mattress, having hoisted me aboard in my litter, and I had to endure three days at sea without eating. Then I spent a few days settling things with M. Tian and left for the hospital where the English doctor advised me, a fortnight later, to push off back to Europe.

I'm absolutely certain that if the pain in the joint had been treated at once, it could easily have been cured and would have had no consequences. But I had no idea how serious it was, and I ruined everything by insisting on long walks and hard work.

Why don't they teach medicine at school, at least enough to prevent people from making such stupid mistakes?

If anyone, in the condition in which I then found myself, came to me for advice, I would say to him: however bad it is, never let them amputate. If you die, it will be better than living with a missing limb. People often refuse, and if I had another chance, I would. Better to suffer the tortures of hell for a year than to let them amputate!

Anyway, they have. And this is the result. Most of the time I'm sitting down, but every so often, I get up, hop a hundred yards or so on my crutches, and then sit down again. My hands can't grip. When I'm walking, I can't take my eyes off my only foot and the end of the crutches. My head and shoulders bend forward and I look like a hunchback. I'm frightened of things and people moving around me, in case they knock me over and break my other leg. People watch me hopping and snigger. When I sit down again, my hands are limp, my armpits are bruised, my expression is vacuous. I despair; and I sit here, completely powerless, snivelling, and waiting for the night, which will bring me the same endless insomnia until the dawn of a day still more miserable than the last. So it goes on.

I will write again soon.

All best wishes,
RIMBAUD

SELECTED BIBLIOGRAPHY

Album Rimbaud: ed. Pierre Petitfils and Henri Matarasso, Bibliothèque de la Pléiade, 1967

Rimbaud: *Oeuvres Complètes,* ed. Roland de Renéville and Jules Mouquet, Bibliothèque de la Pléiade, 1965

Verlaine: *Oeuvres Poétiques Complètes,* ed. Jacques Borel, Bibliothèque de la Pléiade, 1965

Delahaye, Ernest: *Souvenirs Familiers,* Messein, 1925

Lepelletier, Edmond: *Paul Verlaine, sa vie, son oeuvre,* Mercure de France, 1907

Martino, Pierre: *Verlaine,* Boivin, 1924

Mouquet, Jules: *Rimbaud raconté par Verlaine,* Mercure de France, 1934

Porché, François: *Verlaine tel qu'il fut,* Flammarion, 1933

Rimbaud, Isabelle: *Reliques,* Mercure de France, 1922

Starkie, Enid: *Arthur Rimbaud,* Faber & Faber (3rd ed.), 1961

Verlaine, Ex-Madame: *Mémoires de ma vie,* Flammarion, 1935

Wilson, Edmund: *Axel's Castle,* Charles Scribner, 1931 (Fontana, 1961)

TREATS

For PEGGY

I wonder, wonder, who,
Mbee-doo oo who,
Who wrote the book of love.

Lyrics from the song,
'Book Of Love'
(Davis-Patrick-Malone)

– it doesn't take much to see that the problems of three little people don't amount to a hill o' beans in this crazy world.

From the screen play
of Casablanca *by*
Julius J. and Philip G. Epstein
and Howard Koch

Characters:

ANN
PATRICK
DAVE

Ann's flat in London. August, 1974; or now.

Treats was presented at the Royal Court Theatre in February 1976 by the English Stage Company and Michael Codron. The cast was as follows:

DAVE	James Bolam
ANN	Jane Asher
PATRICK	Stephen Moore

Directed by Robert Kidd
Designed by Andrew Sanders
Lighting by Jack Raby

SCENE ONE

The main room of ANN's *flat in London. Rather severely and (for reasons which will emerge) sparsely furnished. The main item of furniture is a full-length, high-backed sofa, facing front, with a coffee-table in front of it. The rest of the room is divided into three principal areas: a dining-recess, with a table and one chair; a desk, facing the window, covered with papers and books; and a white colour-T.V. set facing an uncomfortable-looking modern leather swivel-chair pretty much out of keeping with the rest of the furniture. No carpet: instead a couple of rugs covering rather unexpected areas of the floor. Apart from this, there is a telephone near the desk, a large ornate mirror on the side wall and two sets of bookshelves, one fairly full, the other empty except for two or three volumes, lying on their sides. The main door, which leads into a tiny hall is in the centre of the back wall; and there are two other doors leading to the kitchen and the bedroom respectively. Early evening in autumn.*

ANN, *who is in her mid-twenties and striking rather than beautiful, sits on the sofa, leafing through* Vogue. *Next to her, holding her hand, is* PATRICK. *He is about ten years older, and looks amiable enough, although faintly absurd at present, as he is wearing large white head-phones, connected by a long lead to the amplifier, which is in the fuller of the two bookshelves next to the door. He is listening to the 3rd movement of Bruckner's 4th Symphony, fairly loud, and clearly enjoying himself.*

After a time, he speaks.

PATRICK: Apparently, when Bruckner finally got to hear one of
  his symphonies performed, he was so chuffed he tried to tip
  the conductor.
  (*Brief silence.*)

ANN: How come you know all these things?

PATRICK (*not hearing*): Or so it says on the sleeve. (*As he speaks, he realises* ANN *has said something.*) What?

ANN: Nothing.

(*She smiles. Silence.*)

PATRICK: I think that's rather touching. (*He looks at* ANN, *who is smiling broadly.*) You obviously think it's pathetic.

ANN: Not at all.

PATRICK: What?

(*Longish silence. Then, from outside, quite clearly, the sound of breaking glass.* ANN *looks up, startled.*)

What?

(ANN *shakes her head at him and he sinks back into the music. Ten seconds.* ANN, *looking worried, gets up and starts moving round behind the sofa. As she does so, the handle of the door turns and it begins very slowly to open.* ANN *freezes.* DAVE *appears in the doorway. He is a man of about 30, ordinary enough looking in the normal run of events, but possessed of a kind of malignant energy, which is at the moment particularly apparent.* ANN *seems about to cry out, or at least to speak, but* DAVE *puts his finger to his lips so quickly he succeeds in checking her. He stands for a moment, assessing the scene, then moves swiftly to the amplifier and turns the volume up very loud indeed.* PATRICK *leaps to his feet with a howl of pain, plucking ineffectually at his headphones as if they were a swarm of bees. Finally he manages to get them off and throws them down on the sofa.*)

Christ Jesus!

(*At this moment he becomes aware of* DAVE, *who is already striding purposefully towards him. They come together behind the sofa, where, without the slightest hesitation,* DAVE *punches* PATRICK *very hard on the nose.* PATRICK *collapses behind the sofa, vanishing entirely from view.* ANN *screams.* DAVE *turns and strides back to the amplifier, turns the volume down very low, then turns back to* ANN.)

DAVE: Any messages?

ANN: Get out!

DAVE: Any mail?

ANN: Will you get the hell out of here!

DAVE: That's not very nice.

> (*A groan from* PATRICK. *His hand appears over the back of the sofa.*)

All I want to know is, is there any post for me?

ANN: I sent it on to your mother's.

DAVE: You did what?

> (PATRICK *rises slowly from behind the sofa, very shaken.* DAVE *glances at him briefly, then turns his attention back to* ANN.)

Why?

ANN: I thought you'd be living there for the time being.

PATRICK: Look . . .

DAVE: I thought I was living here for the time being. And if I'm not living here, I'm certainly not going anywhere near that old ginbag. You just sent my letters to her because you know she likes steaming them open. (*Pause. He looks around the room.*) Where's Arthur?

PATRICK: Look . . .

DAVE: Shut up. Where's Arthur?

ANN: I gave him away.

DAVE: What did you say?

ANN: I gave him away.

DAVE: You bitch.

PATRICK: Listen . . .

DAVE: Shut up. Who did you give him to?

ANN: The newsagent.

DAVE: The newsagent?

ANN: Yes, you know, our local newsagent.

DAVE: Well, you listen to me. You better have him back here by this time tomorrow or there'll be trouble.

PATRICK: Now, look here . . .

DAVE: Shut up, you. (*He turns back to* ANN.) Do you understand me?

ANN: If you want him back, you'll have to go and get him yourself.

DAVE: I can't look after him at the moment. Not where I'm staying.

ANN: Then he'll just have to stop where he is. He's perfectly happy there.

153

DAVE: I'm not having my dog dumped off on some bloody wog newsagent. They'll be sending him out delivering before we know where we are.

ANN: Just go away, will you?

DAVE: That is my dog!

ANN: Go away!

DAVE: I'm going to hurt you.

ANN: Call the police, Patrick.

PATRICK: What?

ANN: Call the police.

(PATRICK *begins to move hesitantly towards the telephone.*)

PATRICK: I'm sure . . . Are you sure . . . ?

ANN: He's broken in, assaulted you and threatened me. Tell them that.

PATRICK: 999, is it?

DAVE: Who is this creep?

ANN: Tell them to come right away.

(PATRICK *is now poised above the telephone, eyeing it uneasily.*)

DAVE: I shouldn't pick up that phone if I were you, son.

(PATRICK *picks it up.* DAVE *rushes towards him as he leans forward to dial. Their heads crash. This time it's* DAVE *who has the worst of the encounter. He doubles up and staggers away, moaning and covering his eye.* PATRICK, *startled, stands watching him a moment, then puts the receiver down, concerned.*)

Christ, bloody hell, watch what you're doing.

PATRICK: Sorry.

DAVE: Nearly had my eye out.

PATRICK: I'm very sorry.

DAVE: I should think so.

PATRICK: Are you all right?

DAVE: Fuck.

ANN: Now will you go?

DAVE: Not until you tell me who this strange man is.

ANN: None of your business.

PATRICK: My name is Patrick Archer.

DAVE: Never heard of you.

PATRICK: And you must be Dave Tilley.

154

DAVE: I want to know where you picked him up.

PATRICK: We work together.

ANN: Look, Patrick, will you not stand chatting, I want him to go.

DAVE: Patrick, Patrick, hang on a minute . . . it's not, is it?
    (ANN *avoids his eye, doesn't answer.*)

PATRICK: Not what?

DAVE: Not the famous office bore?

PATRICK: What do you mean?

DAVE: Not the one who's so dull he put that Arab *and* his interpreter to sleep during their meeting?
    (PATRICK *catches* ANN's *eye, then, when she looks away, speaks with some dignity.*)

PATRICK: They'd had a long flight.

DAVE: I can't believe this. I come back from three weeks in Nicosia, most of which I spent lying flat in the corridors of the Ledra Palace Hotel, waiting for some Turk to put a bullet up my Khyber, to find you've not only changed the lock, put my possessions into store and hired some idiot answering service so you don't even have to speak to me, but that you actually appear to be living with a man who's been a household joke for two years. (*To* PATRICK.) You are living here, aren't you? Aren't you married? You look married.

PATRICK: Yes, I am living here; no, I'm not married.

DAVE (*to* ANN): What's the meaning of this?

ANN: The idea was to avoid this kind of scene. After all, we've had enough of them over the last few months.

DAVE: Give me a drink.

ANN: No.

DAVE (*to* PATRICK): Scotch.

ANN: No!

DAVE: It's very probably my Scotch.

ANN: It is not.

DAVE: Look, there are things to discuss, you know, financial matters, that kind of thing. I know you like to pretend none of that exists, but you can't have an amputation without a few bits and bobs need tying up. So why don't we all sit down—(*he does so in the swivel-chair, swivels round to face front*)—and have a drink?

ANN: No.

PATRICK: Let me get him a drink, then you can discuss what you have to discuss and get it over with.

DAVE: That's the boy.

(PATRICK *crosses to the dining-recess, opens a cupboard, takes out a couple of glasses, pours Scotch.* ANN *watches him, annoyed.*)

PATRICK: Like something, love?

ANN: No.

(PATRICK *comes down, hands a glass to* DAVE.)

DAVE: Thanks, thanks. (*He takes a sip.*) It's upset me, punching you like that. I try never to do anything spontaneous.

PATRICK: I'm surprised it was spontaneous.

DAVE: It wasn't, no, in fact I'd planned the whole thing, but the after-effect is the same as if it had been spontaneous.

ANN: I'm going.

DAVE: That's not going to be very helpful.

ANN: Well, then, get on with it.

PATRICK: Do you want *me* to go?

DAVE: Yes.

ANN: No!

DAVE: Make-your-mind-up time.

ANN: Look, it's all settled, everything's settled, so I can't think why you're pissing about. I worked it all out very carefully, so as far as I can see, there's nothing to discuss.

DAVE: Sit down.

(PATRICK *sits on the sofa.* ANN *remains standing.*)

There is, on the contrary, a great deal to discuss, and since you insist on washing our dirty linen in public, let me begin with something which is very near to my heart, not to say directly beneath my bum: namely, my chair.

ANN: What?

DAVE: This is my chair.

ANN: We bought it together.

DAVE: Precisely. For me. We bought it together for me.

ANN: Listen, there are two pieces of furniture we went out and

156

bought together. One was this chair and the other was the rug. And since the rug was considerably more expensive than the chair, I decided if I gave you the rug, you'd have nothing to complain about.

DAVE: The rug.

ANN: Yes.

DAVE: Well, now, that's going to be very handy for sitting at my desk typing, isn't it?

ANN: The desk is mine.

DAVE: I don't mean that ramshackle old heap, I mean *my* desk.

PATRICK: Are you sure you wouldn't rather I went?

ANN: Oh, shut up.

DAVE: If you'd really wanted to be on the safe side, you would have given me the chair and the rug. However, since I'm a reasonable man, I propose you give me the chair and I'll bring you back the rug.

ANN: No, I don't want you bringing it back. Have someone deliver it and collect the chair and send me the bill.

DAVE: Right. Excellent. Now. Next. Fixtures and fittings.

ANN: You want half the curtains?

DAVE: Oh, very good, this is very good. No, no, as you well know, fixtures and fittings has very little to do with the curtains. It's a metaphysical, landlord's idea, the purpose of which was to secure, as you will remember, large and far from metaphysical sums of money.

ANN: You want half the money.

DAVE: Well, I hadn't actually worked it out in detail, but . . . now you mention it, yes, all right, yes, I would like half the money.

ANN: You shit.

DAVE: I wouldn't want to press you or anything, it's just I'm a bit short at the moment.

ANN: I'll give it to you as and when I can get hold of it, I haven't got anything like that kind of money at the moment.

DAVE: Do you wonder the country is on its knees?

ANN: Naturally I'll have to deduct for the pane of glass you broke in the door.

PATRICK: This is awful.

B
157

ANN: Now why don't you go away? I don't know why you have to go through all this. For the last year, you've done nothing but threaten to leave me; all I did was the work.

DAVE: Work? I spent hours in Nicosia lying on my belly in the telephone queue, while you were in bed with a bore of international reputation, you call that work?
(*Silence.* DAVE *suddenly looks defeated, his face collapses.*)
I want . . . to talk to you alone.

ANN: No.

DAVE: I must, it's very important.

ANN: No.

DAVE: Please. Please.
(DAVE *bursts into tears. Longish silence, broken only by his sobs.*)
Ann.

ANN: Don't.

DAVE: You mustn't do this to me, Ann.

ANN: It's too late for all this.

DAVE: I want to go on living with you.

PATRICK: Perhaps I'd better . . .

ANN: No.

DAVE: It's so sudden. You shouldn't have done it just like that.

ANN: Better quick.

DAVE: I'd made up my mind. I'd made up my mind I was going to ask you to marry me when I got back.

ANN: That's not what you said on the phone.

DAVE: I was frightened. I got frightened. In Cyprus. I'd decided. I knew something had to be done.

ANN: Something has been done.

DAVE: Let me come back. I'm sorry. I'm sorry. I know I was . . . I'm . . .

ANN: I really think you must go now.

DAVE: All right.
(*Silence.* DAVE *wipes his eyes, blows his nose, his face re-assembles. He gets up.*)

PATRICK: Would you like me to call you a taxi?

DAVE (*angrily*): I can't afford a taxi, I'm completely broke. (*He subsides, breathes deeply, is now just as he was before breaking down.*) I'll walk.

ANN: Where are you staying?

DAVE: The Savoy.

ANN: That's absurd.

DAVE: None of your bloody business.

ANN: I'm surprised you don't go and stay with one of your mistresses.

DAVE: You know very well all my mistresses in London are married. (*He moves over to the door.*) I'll be in touch.
(ANN *shakes her head.* DAVE *leans round her to smile at* PATRICK.)
Pip pip, old fart.
(*He leaves. Silence.* PATRICK *gets up, moves towards* ANN *as she comes away from the door. She avoids him, sits in the swivel-chair. He hovers a moment, then returns to the sofa, sits down again.*)

ANN: He'll never forgive me now. (*Pause.*) Not that he would have done anyway. (*Pause.*) Jesus.

PATRICK: So that's him.

ANN: Yes.

PATRICK: Can't ever remember such an unusual meeting.

ANN: I told you he was a bastard.

PATRICK: Whatever made you put up with him for so long?
(*Silence.*)

ANN: Expect he'll be back.
(*Silence.*)

PATRICK: Tell me . . . why did you tell him all those things about how boring I was?

ANN: That's the kind of thing he used to enjoy.
(*Silence.*)

PATRICK: Fair enough.

('*Runaway*' *sung by Del Shannon.*)

SCENE TWO

The next morning. Empty stage. The sound of a key in the lock, then
PATRICK *enters, followed by* DAVE, *who looks somewhat the worse for*
wear, but seems cheerful.

DAVE: Well, this is very civil of you, old sport. Any chance of a
    cup of coffee?
PATRICK: Sure.
    (*He moves across the dining-recess and off into the kitchen;*
    clatter of cups. Meanwhile, DAVE *settles himself comfortably in*
    the swivel-chair. PATRICK *reappears.*)
    Where is this undertaker's?
DAVE: Chalk Farm.
PATRICK: Bit out of your way.
DAVE: I decided to go and see a friend. As it turned out, she
    wasn't very pleased to see me. Wasn't my lucky evening for
    social calls.
    (PATRICK *smiles uneasily.*)
    However, she was able to give me a bottle of Scotch.
    Then she made an excuse and I left.
PATRICK: To the undertaker's.
DAVE: Not immediately. I wandered about a bit and drank the
    Scotch. I was just thinking I couldn't possibly make it all
    the way back to the Savoy, when I spotted the shop. Could
    be I'm developing a taste for breaking and entering, anyway
    it was very easy, and I was just settling down for a kip in
    this very comfortable silk-lined casket when they arrested me.
PATRICK: How come?
DAVE: Apparently I left the door open.
PATRICK: It's the first time I've seen in the cells.

DAVE: It's all right. I was past caring. (*Pause.*) I'm sorry I had to get you involved.

PATRICK: That's . . .

DAVE: I couldn't very well tell them I was staying at the Savoy, could I, they'd have given me a proper kicking.

PATRICK: I'll fix the coffee.

(*He exits to the kitchen.* DAVE *turns and shouts after him.*)

DAVE: White please. And white sugar. None of your poncy crystals.

(PATRICK *returns with two mugs of coffee, hands one to* DAVE, *who takes it without acknowledgement, moves across to the sofa, sits, sips. Silence.*)

PATRICK: I believe, I believe we have a friend in common.

(DAVE *looks across at him, waiting.*)

Charles Peters.

DAVE: Charlie.

PATRICK: Yes.

DAVE: Mate of yours, is he?

PATRICK: Well . . .

DAVE: Because he's certainly no friend of mine.

PATRICK: Oh, really?

DAVE: Matter of fact, I think he's a fucking toerag.

PATRICK: Ah.

(*Silence.*)

DAVE: I suppose you have a lot of friends.

PATRICK: Fair number, you know . . .

DAVE: Yes. Don't believe in it myself.

PATRICK: Don't believe in what?

DAVE: Friends. Loyalty I believe in.

PATRICK: I don't um . . .

DAVE: What you going to do, marry her?

PATRICK: Well, I mean, eventually, maybe I yes will possibly.

DAVE: What's she said to you about me?

PATRICK: Enough.

DAVE: What I want to know is, how long have you been lurking around waiting for this to happen? (*Pause.*) Have you spent years admiring her from afar? Or were you the sympathetic shoulder for her to snivel on? Or have you in fact been

161

giving her one twice weekly down amongst the filing
cabinets?

PATRICK: Yes; to a certain extent; and no.

DAVE: What are you talking about?

PATRICK: Answering your questions.

DAVE: I see. (*Pause.*) In that case, what do you mean by to a
certain extent?

PATRICK: I mean I tried to be sympathetic whenever she was
obviously unhappy, which I think she appreciated. But she
never told me what it was was making her unhappy.

DAVE: In other words she never complained about me?

PATRICK: No.

DAVE: That woman has no feelings.

PATRICK: Is that a joke?

DAVE: No, of course it isn't, you humourless berk.

PATRICK: It seems to me . . . if you're frightened what people are
going to say about you, you should be careful how you treat
them.

DAVE: And conversely, needlepoint mottoes can make your
thumb bleed.

(*Silence.* PATRICK, *puzzled.* DAVE, *drinking his coffee.*)
Anyway, was it worth waiting for?

PATRICK: What?

DAVE: What do you think?

PATRICK: I don't think I have to talk to you about that.

DAVE: Reason I ask is, the age I am now, which is of course the
age you were some years ago, can't remember the point of
this remark . . . oh, yes, what I used to regret most were
the women I couldn't have; now, as often as not, it's the
women I do have.

PATRICK: Not a problem of mine.

DAVE: What I mean is, you've had the best of her now, from now
on it'll be downhill all the way. She's not what I'd call sparky,
you'll find it gets pretty boring, I used to have to put a record
on or read a book. Why go through all that and upset yourself? Why don't you leave her to me, I'm all she's good for.

PATRICK: What do you expect me to say to that?

DAVE: Yes.

(*Silence.*)

PATRICK: Look, it's really no good talking to me about all this.

DAVE: I know that, I realise that, but I don't seem to have much alternative, do I? I mean, if you come back from abroad and find the person you've been living with for two and a half years has locked you out and refuses to speak to you, you have to grasp at any straw. Put yourself in my place. (*Pause.*) Mentally, I mean.

PATRICK: I know, well, I tried to persuade Ann this might not be the best way of going about things, but she insisted.

DAVE: You mean she doesn't do what you tell her?

PATRICK: You have a very aggressive way of putting a question.

DAVE: You have a very evasive way of not answering one.

PATRICK: I would have thought in your profession, not having your questions answered was all in a day's work.

DAVE: Right. Whereas for you . . .

PATRICK: That's right.

DAVE: I once frightened a man off by spending an entire evening violently attacking the Jesuits.

PATRICK: Was it a subject close to his heart?

DAVE: No, on the contrary, he knew as little about the Jesuits as I did. But once he'd ventured a tentative protest against some particularly outrageous assertion of mine, of course he was done. Hours of flabby footwork and judicious mumblings against the energy and passion of an apparently committed man. You can imagine the effect on the woman in question.

PATRICK: Yes.

DAVE: The contempt she felt for that poor bastard was something beautiful to behold. Of course, she was very stupid. I married them off in the end. I sometimes wonder how often and in what terms they speak of Jesuits.

PATRICK: Is this by way of being a warning?

DAVE: Only indirectly. The Jesuits wouldn't do for you and Ann. Whereas anything would have done for those two. Stock-car racing. I could have harangued him on stock-car racing, that would have been almost as good. Although the Jesuits did give me more . . .

163

PATRICK: Mileage.

DAVE: Scope. (*Pause.*) Where were you the night I got back, anyway?

PATRICK: Bristol.

DAVE: Bristol?

PATRICK: With my father.

DAVE: Terrific. (*Pause.*) I spent the whole night and most of the next day sitting on my suitcase in the porch.

PATRICK: Didn't you get the letter?

DAVE: Naturally I got the letter. But the letter didn't say you'd be skulking in Bristol for days. Nor did it say you were both going to take a lengthy holiday from the office. By the way, that must have caused some tittle-tattle among your colleagues.

PATRICK: I doubt it.

DAVE: Nor did it say anything about you, beyond referring to you as 'someone else', a more or less accurate but I thought not altogether flattering description. The only way I could find out who you were was to go and listen in to the tittle-tattle among your colleagues.

PATRICK: I see.

DAVE: I'm sorry I pretended not to know who you were last night. I thought it would be . . .

PATRICK: Jesuitical.

DAVE: Expedient, yes. Forgive me. But, you see, you can surely appreciate, it was a desperate situation. I mean, God knows, I've split up with enough people in the past, but it's always been a kind of ritual disembowelling. Never the guillotine.

PATRICK: Ann thought it would be better.

DAVE: Do you?

PATRICK: Well, I must say, judging by the image you've just . . .

DAVE: Then let me put it another way: it's always been a jump but there's usually been a parachute.

PATRICK: Well . . . listen . . . perhaps . . . you should come and have dinner with us this evening.

DAVE: Really?

PATRICK: Yes, I can understand . . . it would be a chance to clear things up.

DAVE: What time?

164

PATRICK: Eightish?

DAVE: Done. (*Pause.*) Ann'll be pleased.

PATRICK: Well, if she really doesn't think it's a good idea, I can always call you and cancel.

DAVE: Yes.

PATRICK: At the Savoy.

DAVE: Oh, yes.

PATRICK: Or at the paper?

DAVE: No, at the Savoy.

PATRICK: Good.

DAVE: My word, this is civilized. Now all that remains is for me to touch you for a loan.

PATRICK: I don't think so.

DAVE: No?

PATRICK: How much do you need?

DAVE: How much can you spare?

PATRICK: As far as I can gather from Ann, you make a great deal more money than I do.

DAVE: Yes, but I need a lot of money.

PATRICK: What for?

DAVE: To spend. What do you think for? To spend.

PATRICK: I see.

DAVE: You think you're underpaid?

PATRICK: Sometimes.

DAVE: Perhaps you should become a miner.

PATRICK: What?

DAVE: I'm sorry, it's just something I say to test people's reactions. If they laugh, I know they're shits.

PATRICK: I might easily have laughed. Out of politeness, say.

DAVE: Makes no difference, does it?

(*Silence.* PATRICK's *hand goes to his inside pocket.*)

PATRICK: I . . . could probably manage something, just to . . . tide you over.

DAVE: Well. That's very handsome.

PATRICK: Erm . . .

DAVE: But no.

PATRICK: No?

DAVE: No, on mature reflection, I don't think it would be right.

165

PATRICK: Just as you like.

DAVE: Thanks all the same. Very generous of you. Shows there are more important things in life than women.

PATRICK: Ann tells me you hate women.

DAVE: She's a clever girl.

PATRICK: Why is that?

DAVE: My mum wouldn't let me have a bicycle.

PATRICK: I see.

(*Silence.* PATRICK *gets up, looks at his watch, hovers indeterminately for a few seconds.*)

DAVE: Anything I can do for you?

PATRICK: Well. I'm afraid I have to go. I'm very late as it is.

DAVE: Don't let me keep you.

PATRICK: I thought . . .

DAVE: I just have to make one or two phone calls, if that's all right. In lieu of the loan.

PATRICK: Well, all right.

DAVE: I know you have to get on. This country may be on its knees, but others are on their faces in the mud, am I right?

PATRICK: Close . . . the door behind you.

DAVE: I've lived here for years, I know how to close the door.

PATRICK: Yes.

DAVE: See you this evening. You are going to be here this evening?

PATRICK: Yes, of course.

DAVE: Just wondered.

(*Silence.* PATRICK *moves uncertainly towards the door.*)

How's your nose?

PATRICK: What?

DAVE: Your nose. (*He mimes swinging a punch.*)

PATRICK: Oh, fine, thanks.

DAVE: Terrific. (*Pause.*) Thanks for everything.

(PATRICK *nods awkwardly, confused; and exits.* DAVE *calls out after him.*)

Take care. (*He grins to himself, gets up, crosses to the desk and begins to rummage purposefully through the papers and letters.*)

('*It's a Wonderful World*' *sung by Louis Armstrong.*)

166

SCENE THREE

An hour or two later. DAVE *alone, still at the desk. He holds a bundle of letters in one hand, and in the other hand a single letter, which he is reading. After a time, he grunts, replaces the pile of letters on the desk, pauses, reflects, looks at his watch, takes a small diary out of his top pocket and crosses to the telephone. He looks a number up, dials and waits.*

DAVE (*North Country accent*): 'Ello. Could I have the electrical department, please? . . . the electrical department . . . oh, is it? . . . oh, beg your pardon, mate, sorry . . . tara. (*He puts the receiver down, riffles through his diary, dials again, waits. This time, he speaks with his normal accent.*) Hello, Emma? . . . this is Dave . . . yes . . . yes, I know . . . what you up to this afternoon? . . . well, I thought you might like to pop round and visit me at the Savoy . . . that's right . . . oh . . . can't you put them off? . . . oh, well, never mind, perhaps next week sometime . . . well, I'm not sure, I'll ring you nearer the time . . . O.K., love, have to run now . . . yes . . . speak to you soon . . . bye. (*He puts the receiver down, turns to another page in the diary, puts his hand out towards the phone, hesitates, then picks up the receiver, dials a number, waits.*) Hello . . . yes, that's right . . . well, I've been away . . . Cyprus . . . can you make lunch? . . . (*With some relief.*) Well, then, this afternoon . . . well, get your mother round . . . about three would be good . . . the Savoy . . . the Savoy Hotel . . . in the Strand . . . I don't know what tube it is, get a taxi, I'll pay you back . . . yes, ask for me at the desk . . . bring your wellies and half a pound of butter . . . it's a joke . . . yes, all right . . . all right, love, see you later.

(He puts the receiver down, sighs, puts his diary back in his top pocket, smooths his hair, crosses to the mirror, combs his hair, puts his comb away, rubs his chin, studies himself in the mirror. He stands looking at himself for some time, expressionless. Then he moves to the bookshelf, looks through the records and selects the Bob Dylan L.P. 'Nashville Skyline'. He switches on the record-player, puts the record on and sets the needle down carefully at the beginning of the track 'I Threw It All Away'. Then he sits down to listen to it. When the song finishes, he gets up quickly and moves the needle back to the beginning of the track, and, as the song begins again, returns to the mirror.)

SCENE FOUR

ANN, PATRICK *and* DAVE *sit round the dining-table*—ANN *on a kitchen-stool,* PATRICK *on the chair from in front of the desk and* DAVE *on the regular straight-backed chair. On the table, the remains of their dinner.*
    Enormous silence.

DAVE: Did you know, I think this might interest you, Patrick, as
    a detail of some consequence in the history of your new
    home, that Dwight D. Eisenhower slept here?

PATRICK: Did he?

DAVE: Well, he came to a lot of meetings.

PATRICK: Is that true?

ANN: Of course not, you buffoon.
    (*Silence.*)

DAVE: This the kind of evening you normally spend?

PATRICK: What do you mean?

DAVE: Well, you know, full of fun.

ANN: We don't normally spend our evenings under the
    malignant eye of a drunken journalist.

DAVE: You mean, Patrick doesn't.

ANN: Nor do we usually spend our evenings with people who've
    had specific messages left for them, telling them not to come.

DAVE: Very remiss, those boys at reception.

ANN: Why didn't you answer your phone all afternoon?

DAVE: *A* because I was busy and *b* because I knew you would
    call.
    (*Silence.*)
    I must say, that was a better bloody meal than you ever
    cooked me. Tell you what, why don't you move out and I'll
    live with Patrick. Mm? You could get somewhere cosy

round the corner and Patrick and I could pop round to see you alternate evenings. After dinner. Then, you never know, one night, Patrick and I might strike it lucky and we need trouble you no further.

(*Silence.* DAVE *gets up and moves into the body of the room.*)

Well, mine's a small coffee and a large brandy.

ANN: You've had your free meal, now piss off.

DAVE: But, Ann, the discussion, Ann, our discussion.

ANN: What's to discuss?

DAVE: Oh, dearie me.

(*Silence.* PATRICK *rises.*)

PATRICK: I'll fix the coffee.

DAVE: I want this man to be the mother of my children.

(PATRICK *steps into the kitchen, carrying plates.* DAVE *moves to the bookshelf, starts looking through the records. Silence.* DAVE *fetches out a John Lennon L.P.*)

This is mine.

ANN: It is not.

DAVE: Well, look, I don't want to make an issue of it, but it is in fact mine.

ANN: All right, take it.

DAVE: No, if you want it, of course, I wouldn't dream of taking it.

ANN: I don't want the bloody thing, take it.

DAVE: O.K.

(DAVE *puts it in one of the empty bookshelves, facing front.* PATRICK *comes out of the kitchen with a tray, puts it on the coffee-table in front of the sofa, arranges the cups. As he does so, the sound of chanting voices in the distance, indistinct at first, then swelling, so that the phrase 'Send them back' can be discerned.*)

PATRICK: What's that?

DAVE: Demonstration.

PATRICK: National Front?

DAVE: I.R.A. (*He gestures vaguely.*) The Home Secretary lives over there somewhere.

(*The chant changes to one of 'Murderer' which is heard clearly for a few seconds before beginning to die away to a murmur.* DAVE, *meanwhile, has a glint in his eye, as a thought strikes him.*)

Course it's nothing compared to the man downstairs.

PATRICK: The man downstairs?

DAVE: What, you mean to say you haven't heard the man downstairs? Practising his trombone? Listen, you have to be as insensitive as a warthog, like me, or more so, like Ann, to be able to put up with the man downstairs. I should have thought any normal person would find living over him absolutely intolerable. A few rounds of 'Twinkle, twinkle, little star' on that thing, and you'll be . . .

ANN: Give up.

DAVE: Who's that? My God, you gave me a fright, I'd forgotten you were here.

ANN: We all know our neighbour downstairs is a very sweet old lady.

DAVE: Are you going to sit on that penitential stool all evening? It's going to make our discussion unnecessarily diffuse.

(ANN *doesn't move.* DAVE, *who has helped himself to coffee, settles himself comfortably in the swivel-chair, and turns to* PATRICK.)

PATRICK: Erm. . . ?

DAVE: There is some brandy, isn't there?

PATRICK: Yes.

(PATRICK *fetches some brandy, pours a glass in the dining-recess, exchanging a glance with* ANN.)

DAVE: Large as you like.

(PATRICK *takes the glass over to him, sits down on the sofa.*)
Now.

(DAVE *takes a sip, pauses.* ANN *gets up and crosses to the sofa, sits next to* PATRICK, *pours herself some coffee.*)
Patrick.

PATRICK: Yes.

DAVE: Where do you live?

PATRICK: Here.

DAVE: Yes, I know that, I'm not talking about now, I mean usually.

PATRICK: Oh, at my mother's.

DAVE: Really? Do you mean with your mother?

PATRICK: Yes.

DAVE: Amazing.

PATRICK: Well, it's a big house. That's to say, I have a floor to myself. When my parents divorced, my mother kept the house in London.

DAVE: Good housekeeper, eh?

PATRICK: What?

DAVE: Nothing.

PATRICK: Oh, I see.

DAVE: So, divorced. I'm surprised. My old man died last year after 37 years of ecstatically happy marriage. Least, he'd spent so long telling everyone it was ecstatically happy, I think dying was the only method he could devise of getting out of it gracefully.

ANN: If we're quite up-to-date with each other's family histories, perhaps now we could move on to the weather.

DAVE: Look, I'm just trying to get a full picture of the situation.

ANN: Patrick's former domestic arrangements, if I may say so, have bugger all to do with the situation.

DAVE: Well, you never know, I thought he might have a nice cheap flat to rent me. Naturally, now I know it's a question of moving in with his mother, I shall have to think again, no disrespect to the poor old cow. (*Pause.*) Also, I couldn't help noticing there's nothing here that doesn't belong to you or, as for example in the case of this chair, me. And that made me curious.

PATRICK: Well . . .

DAVE: What I mean is, don't you find it inconvenient having to go back to your mother's every time you want to change your socks?

PATRICK: I have my clothes here. I've never accumulated very much in the way of possessions.

DAVE: Yes, well, very commendable. But you see now why I've been pursuing this tack. I mean, I can't really be blamed for thinking it all looks a bit temporary. Can I?

ANN: You can be blamed for mixing it, which is what you're up to. If there's anything to discuss, which there isn't, it's not

172

to do with Patrick. It's to do with why I decided to do what I have done, and what took me so long about it.

DAVE: All right, let's talk about that.

(*Silence.*)

Well, go on.

ANN: What's there to say, except that for two and a half years you bullied and terrorized me to such an extent I could hardly open my mouth. I didn't dare to have an opinion you hadn't approved about anything. My friends pitied me and your friends despised me. The only peace I ever had was when you were away, and even then you were ringing up every evening snarling and taunting and threatening me about something or other. How's that to be kicking off with?

DAVE: Yes, well, I'm not denying it. I have erred. You're quite right. I have in fact erred.

ANN: And that's not to mention that in the course of those two and a half years you had affairs or at any rate sexual relations with forty-two other women.

DAVE: Oh, you counted?

ANN: No, you counted. I don't know or care whether you tell the truth about these things, but the mathematics is yours.

DAVE: I see.

ANN: And judging by what I've been told since, things were not always as you described them.

DAVE: Told by whom? What have you been told? What do you mean?

ANN: All I mean is people say just as unpleasant and probably more accurate things about you behind your back as you say about them behind theirs.

DAVE (*to* PATRICK): Doesn't speak very well, does she?

ANN: And don't start that again.

DAVE: Sorry.

ANN: Don't you bloody start on that again.

DAVE: All right.

ANN: He used to save up clumsy sentences I'd said, and repeat them to me when we got home.

PATRICK: You told me.

ANN: Well, I'm telling you again, it's relevant, isn't it?

C

173

PATRICK: Yes, I know, I'm not saying you told me, I don't want
to hear it again, I'm saying you told me, I know about it
and I can see why you said it.

DAVE: Your sentences aren't too elegant either, are they? (*Pause.*)
However, I suppose grammar is the least of our worries.

ANN: Ha.

DAVE: Two of those and you'd be laughing.

(ANN *scowls,* PATRICK *laughs;* ANN *looks at him coldly.*)

ANN: Enjoying yourself?

DAVE: Well, much more than I did during dinner. But then, if
somebody'd thrown up it would have been a relief.

ANN: I was speaking to Patrick.

PATRICK: Oh.

DAVE: Let's leave Patrick out of it for the moment, shall we, and
see if we can't get back to what we were talking about. Our
relationship. Now you were saying, if I read you correctly,
that I bullied you and never allowed you to have any
opinions of your own.

ANN: Yes.

DAVE: Not true. When we met, you actually *had* no opinions of
your own. Consequently, as time went on, the opinions you
picked up tended to be mine, and if they weren't, they were
sufficiently shaky and newly established to crumble as soon as
I attacked them. Do you think I liked that? Do you think I
liked hearing you parrot out all the things I'd told you to
everyone we met? Do you think I liked the fact it was
impossible to have an argument with you about any subject
however neutral without you taking it personally? It's
possible to disagree with someone about the ethics of
non-violence without wanting to kick his face in. All that
mute suffering you used to go through whenever we'd had
some piddling dispute about the Common Market or the
Stock Market or the supermarket or some other damn
thing we didn't in fact give a toss about. I much prefer you
the way you are now if you want to know.

ANN: Nonsense, if I ever argued with you about anything, you
used to go berserk. In the end, I just stopped bothering.

DAVE: I said I much prefer you the way you are now.

ANN: I heard you. The only reason for that is you aren't living with me. If you were living with someone, you'd go home tonight and tell her how wonderful I was and abuse her for not being more like me.

DAVE: I never realised you felt so resentful about the other women.

ANN: Didn't you, I thought that was half the fun.

DAVE: You never seemed to mind very much. Except your friend whatshername, but that was a bit different. I mean, that's what we agreed at the beginning, isn't it, freedom and honesty. We could do what we liked as long as we didn't have to tell lies about it. Isn't that what we agreed?

ANN: It's what you announced. I never believed for a moment that sort of freedom was supposed to apply to me.

DAVE: You didn't want it.

ANN: That's not the point, is it?

DAVE: Of course it's the point, it's not my fault if you're temperamentally unpromiscuous, or however it was you described it.

ANN: Anyway, if you're so bloody liberal, why did you split my lip that day I had lunch with Justin?

DAVE: I took against his name.

ANN: Then why didn't you split his lip?

DAVE: He's bigger than you are.

ANN: Very funny.

DAVE: What I want to know is, if I'm so appalling, how come you put up with me for so long?

ANN: That's a really stupid question.

PATRICK: Sounds fair enough to me.

ANN: Oh, does it?

PATRICK: Well, yes.

ANN: Then you answer it.

PATRICK: I can't answer it.

ANN: Then don't interrupt.

DAVE: Don't be horrible to Patrick.

ANN: What are you up to?

DAVE: What do you mean?

ANN: Why are you pretending to be so nice?

DAVE: I'm not pretending to be anything, I'm just sitting here waiting for the answer to a perfectly simple question.

ANN: And I'm just sitting here waiting for you to piss off home.

DAVE: You see, Patrick, how years of living with me have taken their toll. She used to be so docile.

PATRICK: Really?

DAVE: Now I find that in leaving me she's taken with her several of my most unpleasant characteristics.

PATRICK: I wouldn't go so far as to say that.

DAVE: He's a goer, isn't he?

ANN: Dave, there are two of us here. I don't know why you persist in speaking to us one at a time.

DAVE: Divide and rule.

ANN: That's what I thought.

DAVE: All right then, since I've been unmasked, I may as well come to the point of this discussion, and I'll try and address it to both of you, although of course that was not at all my intention, and what I'm saying is for you and not for Patrick. I've always lived, privately and professionally, according to very simple principles, you know, with money and women, if in doubt say yes, with friends and neighbours, if in doubt say no, there's no business like show business, never trust a politician beginning with K, that kind of uncomplicated and reliable rule of thumb. I mean, I watch a few people doing their bit and thinking they'll stop the rot, but, like the majority, I don't really see much point in trying to dig steps in the side of the whirlpool. Better to go down smiling. So you'll appreciate that what I'm about to say is a betrayal of all my deepest instincts. Will you marry me?

ANN: What?

DAVE: Will you marry me?

ANN: Can I have a moment to think about it?

DAVE: No.

ANN: In that case, the answer is no.

DAVE: All right, you can have a moment to think about it.

(ANN *thinks for a moment. Silence.*)

ANN: No.

176

DAVE: Look, if it's the women, if you're still worried about the women, I think I might be able to offer you certain concessions. I mean, most of the time, I can't say I enjoyed it all that much, having to put up with all their blather and misery, but I made sacrifices, you know, as we all have to. I think I could promise you to break all the, what, emotional entanglements, at any rate.

ANN: It's not the women.

DAVE: Well, what is it then?

ANN: It's you.

DAVE: I'm just explaining to you, I've decided to change.

ANN: Oh, come on, next thing you're going to say is, you're only a humble reporter.

DAVE: Ann, this is less than reasonable. I don't think you're being quite fair.

ANN: What's anything to do with fair, as you used to say.

DAVE: Patrick, I appeal to you now, I appeal to you as a neutral observer.

PATRICK: Hardly neutral.

DAVE: No, I know, but you know what I mean. What I mean is, is this right?

PATRICK: Seems perfectly all right to me. You asked her to marry you and she said no.

DAVE: No, Patrick, I don't think you're really with me. (*Pause.*) Look, let me give you a simple illustration of what we're talking about. There's a girl works at the paper, has the most enormous tits.

ANN: Jesus.

DAVE: No, no, bear with me. You'll see the relevance of this in a moment. (*To* PATRICK.) Anyway, there she is, otherwise totally unremarkable, except, as I say, for these truly massive knockers. Well, one day, when Ann was away, I could restrain myself no further, and I invited her out to dinner. Afterwards, I brought her back here, and, after the usual dreary two hours of blabbing away, I managed to get her to bed. Once there, I confessed to her that all I really wanted to do, and indeed all I intended to do was to satisfy my curiosity as to the appearance and texture of her

absolutely mesmerizing and exorbitant dongers. I just
wanted to gaze, assess and generally fondle. Fortunately,
she took it like a trouper and we're still the best of friends.
Now, what I'm driving at, Patrick, is that that pleasant
incident can't possibly have done the slightest harm to the
girl, to me or to Ann, can it? Am I right or am I right?

ANN: If I've heard about that poor wretched girl's tits once . . .

DAVE: Now, now, I'm asking Patrick. Fair dos.

ANN: Fair dos!

DAVE: What do you think, Patrick?

PATRICK: Well. I'm not sure what . . . I mean, by and large . . .
as a course of action in itself, I wouldn't particularly
approve of it, but . . . you see, I don't know what your
arrangement was with Ann, and if . . . that was your
arrangement, I suppose there was no harm in it. I'm not
sure I know what you're driving at.

DAVE: What I'm driving at is, that was the kind of thing that
was held against me.

PATRICK: I see.

DAVE: That was the kind of thing she meant when she said I
terrorized and bullied her.

PATRICK: Well, if that's the case, and I can't see how you should
suppose I'd be in a position to judge whether it is or not,
but if it is, and I still don't understand why you should
want to ask my opinion about it, if it is, I suppose you're
right.

(*Silence. During this last exchange,* ANN *has been looking
incredulously from one to the other.*)

Personally, I've never really liked them all that enormous
myself.

ANN: Patrick.

PATRICK: Yes.

ANN: I want you to do something for me. I want you to get in
your car and drive Dave to a pub or a strip-club or somewhere, anywhere, away from here, so you can carry on your
anatomical reminiscences with complete abandon. I've got
other things to do. I can't think why you wanted to arrange
this abysmal occasion in the first place, but since you did, I

think it's up to you to get him out of here before he gets
properly launched on the unending saga of his grubby
love-life. Is that clear? There's no point gawping at me like
that, I've made my mind up and I've had enough and I
want you both out of here now.

(PATRICK *stirs uneasily, then subsides.* DAVE *permits himself a
discreet smile.* ANN *looks from one to the other with mounting
annoyance.*)

Go on, go!

(*Silence. Nobody moves.*)

(*'Book of Love' sung by the Monotones.*)

INTERVAL

SCENE FIVE

The next morning. The John Lennon L.P. has vanished from the bookcase.

PATRICK, *alone, sitting on the sofa, looking through some papers, sipping at a cup of coffee. The radio is on, an early morning news bulletin, of which* PATRICK *takes no notice whatsoever, unless a particularly appalling piece of news catches his attention briefly. He puts down the papers, finishes his coffee, looks at his watch, reacts, exits hurriedly to the kitchen. Sounds of washing-up. He crosses to the mirror, checks his tie, starts to move away from the mirror, stops, looks at himself again, dismayed, then exits to the bedroom. He returns a moment later doing up a minimally different tie. He finishes tying it in front of the mirror, then his hand moves to his chin as he notices he is unshaven. Back to the bedroom, to return with a battery shaver, already running. He shaves in front of the mirror, shining his shoes on the back of his trousers as he does so. He turns off the shaver, checks his chin dubiously, then puts the shaver into the briefcase which stands ready by the hall door. He looks at his watch again, then dives into the hall and returns a moment later, struggling into a light raincoat. He picks up the briefcase, stands thinking, then puts the briefcase down and crosses to the dining-recess, where he stands for a moment peering out of the window. He opens the window and stretches his arm out. Then he closes the window and hurries across the room, exiting to the hall. A moment later, he re-appears to fetch his briefcase, holding an umbrella. He picks up his briefcase, stands for a moment, a strained expression on his face, then exits by the hall door. The front door slams. Sound of receding footsteps. Silence. Sound of returning footsteps. Key in the lock.* PATRICK *re-enters. He crosses to the sofa, puts down his umbrella, picks up the papers, fumbles them into his briefcase, picks up his umbrella and strides out to the hall, closing the door behind him. The*

door instantly re-opens, he appears, puts down his umbrella, crosses to
the radio and switches it off. Back to the hall door, where he pauses,
turns to contemplate the room and pats at his pockets with his free
hand, making a final check. Then he exits, leaving his umbrella
behind. The front door slams.

('*Little Darlin*' ' *sung by The Diamonds.*)

SCENE SIX

That evening. ANN, *alone, curled up in the swivel-chair, facing front, reading. She looks up, thoughtfully, as she hears the key in the door. Presently* PATRICK *enters, somewhat wet.*

PATRICK: Hello. (*He looks around.*) Where are you?

ANN: Here.

PATRICK: Oh.

> (*He exits into the hall, peeling off his raincoat, having dropped his briefcase just inside the door.* ANN *swivels round slowly.*)

ANN: Where are you?

PATRICK (*off*): Taking off my coat.

ANN: Ah.

> (PATRICK *re-enters, smoothing his hair. He smiles at* ANN. *Hiatus. Then he bends and fumbles with his briefcase, finally producing a record in a record shop carrier bag.*)

PATRICK: I bought you a present.

ANN: What is it?

> (*She gets up.* PATRICK *holds out the carrier bag.*)

PATRICK: Guess.

ANN: Erm, bunch of daffodils.

PATRICK: No.

ANN: Too difficult, I give up.

PATRICK: It's a record!

ANN: Never.

> (PATRICK *hands it to her, and, as she takes it, tries to kiss her, but bungles it.* ANN *slips the record out of the carrier bag. It is the John Lennon L.P.*)

> (*Coolly.*) Thanks.

PATRICK: It is the one, isn't it?

ANN: What?

PATRICK: The one Dave took.

ANN: Yes. Yes, it is. Very sweet of you.

PATRICK: You do like it, don't you?

ANN: Yes, it's, yes.

PATRICK: I don't think I know it myself.

(ANN *moves to the bookshelves, files the record, disposes of the carrier bag.*)

ANN: Thank you.

PATRICK: Bad move, eh?

ANN: Well, if it's supposed to be making up for last night's fiasco, perhaps it is a bit tactless.

PATRICK: Perhaps so.

ANN: But it was very thoughtful of you.

PATRICK: I'm very sorry about last night.

ANN: Yes, I know, don't let's talk about it.

PATRICK: It's just I thought perhaps he had the right . . .

ANN: That bastard has no rights.

PATRICK: After all, he did ask you to marry him.

ANN: That was a laugh, wasn't it?

PATRICK: Well, I don't know.

ANN: No, you don't, and you shouldn't, it's none of your business.

PATRICK: I suppose not. But, I mean, I wouldn't like to think you'd get rid of me like that. Not without talking it over at all.

ANN: Well . . . (*She breaks off. Pause.*) Your mother phoned.

PATRICK: Oh, did she?

ANN: She wants you to call her back.

PATRICK: Oh. (*He moves towards the phone, then checks himself.*) I'll do it later.

ANN: Do it now if you like.

PATRICK: Later will do.

(*Silence.*)

Busy day?

ANN: Not remotely.

PATRICK: I came down to see you this afternoon, but Jane said you'd slipped out for something.

ANN: There was so little doing today, I amused myself drafting a letter of resignation.

PATRICK: What?

ANN: I think I've had enough.

PATRICK: But . . . you haven't said anything about it before.

ANN: I only drafted the letter, I didn't send it.

PATRICK: All the same. This is a bit of a bombshell.

ANN: I'm fed up with it there. It's true what Dave always used to say. Those people don't need an interpreter. They know perfectly well what they're saying to each other: nothing. I told you last week when I went out to lunch with Morrison and that Spaniard, all Morrison wanted to know was what the investment situation would be like when Franco died.

PATRICK: Yes, well, Dave told me all we were doing was purveying to our hapless brothers overseas the educational ideas that had brought this country to its knees. It's very easy to be cynical.

ANN: Dave's not cynical, he's puritanical.

PATRICK: I very much doubt that.

ANN: Of course he is.

PATRICK: I don't see how he can afford to be.

ANN: The first time I met him, I asked him what he did and he told me he wrote blistering reports in words of not more than one syllable in sentences of not more than five words for a newspaper that was guaranteed not to let the vinegar through.

PATRICK: I thought he worked for um . . .

ANN: Yes, now he says he's allowed to write very considered and interesting articles and all he has to contend with is the fact that nobody reads them.

PATRICK: I don't really see what Dave's problems have to do with your . . .

ANN: Nothing.

PATRICK: Anyway, I thought we weren't allowed to talk about him.

ANN: What do you mean?

PATRICK: Well, every time I mention his name, you bite my head off.

184

ANN: That's because you will insist on talking about him all the time, when you don't know the first thing about him. Not to mention defending him, that's what really gets up my nose.

PATRICK: I don't think I do, do I? It's just . . . I mean, I don't exactly like him, but I certainly don't mind him. I suppose you're right, I suppose I don't know all that much about him.

ANN: Then shut up about him.

(*Silence.*)

PATRICK: All right, tell me why you want to leave the job.

ANN: Because I want to leave you.

(*Silence.*)

PATRICK: No.

(ANN *nods.*)

You don't mean it.

ANN: Yes.

PATRICK: But why?

(*No answer.* PATRICK *has an idea.*)

Oh.

ANN: No.

PATRICK: You want to . . .

ANN: No, I do not. I knew you were going to say that.

PATRICK: You don't.

ANN: I wouldn't dream of it.

PATRICK: Oh. (*Pause.*) Well, you must admit, it's the obvious conclusion.

ANN: It's the obvious conclusion for a man, that one could only bear to leave him in order to go back to some other bloody man.

PATRICK: No, I didn't quite mean it like that. I meant, after seeing him again last night, that is, after seeing both of us together, it might have made you, you know, reawakened some, you know . . .

ANN: The only thing it reawakened was a very strong and urgent desire to live on my own again.

PATRICK: I see.

ANN: That was my mistake, Patrick, that was the mistake, I

185

thought the only way to escape from Dave was to go off with somebody else. I used you. I'm very sorry about it.

PATRICK: Don't apologise, I'm very glad you . . . (*Pause.*) Anyway, don't you think this is all a bit radical after one bad evening?

ANN: No.

PATRICK: After all, you put up with Dave for two and a half years, it seems a bit hard to give me the elbow on the basis of a single sticky dinner-party.

ANN: You know I'm very decisive.

PATRICK: I don't call that decisive, I call it rash.

ANN: How would you know, it takes you forty-five minutes every morning to decide which shoes to put on. And you've only got three pairs.

PATRICK: Well, I . . . (*He breaks off, stares morosely at his feet.*)

ANN: I know it's a very trivial example, but that's the kind of thing I mean.

PATRICK: I may not know what shoes to put on, but I know what I want.

ANN: You don't.

PATRICK: Of course I do, you can't say that, I should know, shouldn't I?

ANN: You have wants the way other people have toothache. Kind of dull and general.

PATRICK: Look, are we talking about what I want, or are we talking about what you want?

ANN: We're talking about what I want, and what I want I want because as far as I can see you don't want anything at all.

PATRICK: Let's have that again.

ANN: You know perfectly well what I mean. You're so cautious and rational, anything as crude as a wish or a whim or a desire dies before you ever get your mouth open.

PATRICK: Balls.

ANN: Patrick.

PATRICK: Well . . .
      (*Silence.*)

ANN: You know something, I think this is the first argument we've ever had.

PATRICK: It isn't.

ANN: It is.

(PATRICK *considers this a moment.*)

PATRICK: Is it?

ANN: Oh, God.

PATRICK: Wait, I'm just trying to think . . .

(*He does so. Silence.*)

We did have that disagreement about Chinese
restaurants, remember?

ANN: Oh, for God's sake, what difference does it make?

PATRICK: Well, it obviously does make a difference, since you're
reproaching me for it.

ANN: No, I'm not, all I meant, the only point I was trying to
make, was you must admit the whole thing has been rather
passionless, joyless . . .

PATRICK: Painless.

ANN: Yes.

PATRICK: Mm, I suppose that probably is my fault. At any rate,
it's a familiar complaint. Someone else once accused me of
being too happy.

ANN: I don't see what that's got to do with it.

PATRICK: Well, by and large it's true that I'm a . . . happy man.
Consequently, I don't expect anything very much from
people, and consequently, I never quite know what it is they
expect from me. To that extent, I'm totally maladjusted.
That's why I find people, or at any rate women, so
bewildering.

ANN: You make a distinction, do you, between women and
people?

PATRICK: No, don't let's get off on all that, you know what I
mean. I mean, when someone says to me, I want this or
that, or I feel this or that, I always try to respond
accordingly. And it's only later I realise that's not what was
meant at all. I'm an incurable optimist, that's the misery of
it.

ANN: An optimist? In this country? Now?

PATRICK: Yes, yes, I know it's all terrible at the moment, but I
believe, I honestly believe, that in a hundred years' time or

maybe two, all those problems, that's to say all the problems that can be, will be sorted out, more or less, and people will be able to start actually doing something with their lives.

ANN: You mean, when we're dead?

PATRICK: Yes.

ANN: You call that optimism?

PATRICK: Yes.

ANN: Well, whatever may or may not be the truth of these philosophical speculations, the fact remains, I've had enough. I've made a mistake and I'm very sorry and now I've had enough.

PATRICK: Right.

(*Silence.*)

ANN: If you were even vulnerable . . .

PATRICK: I'm sure I bleed as much as the next man.

ANN: Maybe you do: but very neatly, I suspect.

(*Silence.* PATRICK *suddenly plunges a hand up his trouser-leg, scratches his calf vigorously.*)

PATRICK: Excuse me scratching, terrible itch.

(ANN *watches him in silence.*)

Shall I, shall I not stay the night? Tonight.

ANN: I don't really see the point, do you?

PATRICK: Oh. Well, then, perhaps I had better ring mother.

ANN: Please yourself.

(*Silence.* PATRICK *gets up. By this time,* ANN *is looking at him with something approaching horror.*)

PATRICK: This is all . . . very painful for me.

ANN (*coldly*): I'm sorry.

PATRICK: Reason I haven't . . . I mean, I don't want you to think it doesn't matter to me . . . it's just . . . the things we were talking about . . . I mean, you're everything *I* want . . . but what *you* want . . . I don't think I could ever . . .

ANN (*much warmer*): What do you mean?

PATRICK: You know . . . maybe I've misunderstood . . . I just wanted to make it clear . . . (*He breaks off, gropes around in his pocket, produces a key-ring.*) I'd better leave your key.

ANN: Don't bother.

(PATRICK *starts trying to get the key off the key-ring. He finds it very difficult. He tugs and fumbles at it with fierce determination.*)

Don't bother.

(PATRICK *perseveres, his face contorted with effort. Finally, he manages to wrench it free.*)

PATRICK: There we are.

ANN: You really needn't have bothered. Not right this minute.

PATRICK: Are you sure? (*He looks down at key and key-ring, begins to draw them together.*)

ANN: Oh, leave it, now you've got it off, I couldn't bear to sit here and have to watch you fiddling the bloody thing on again.

PATRICK: All right. Erm. . . ?

ANN: What?

PATRICK: Where would you like me to leave it?

ANN: Anywhere.

(PATRICK *stands, holding the key, looking uncertainly around the room, from one possible location to another.*)

('*Why Do Fools Fall In Love?*' *sung by Frankie Lymon and The Teenagers.*)

SCENE SEVEN

Two weeks later. Afternoon. Empty stage. ANN *enters from the hall, backwards, protesting, followed by* DAVE, *who has a large rug rolled up over his shoulder. They advance into the room.*

DAVE: Right, where d'you want it, missis?

ANN: I told you not to bring it round yourself.

DAVE: Well, you can't get the labour, guv'nor. (*He drops it off his shoulder on to the floor.*) Jesus, that's heavy. Give us a hand. (*He starts unrolling it, looks up at* ANN.) Come on, shift yourself.
(ANN *moves to help him. They unroll it and begin manoeuvring it into position.*)
Where's Patrick?

ANN: Out.

DAVE: No, he isn't.

ANN: Well, if you know, why ask?

DAVE: Just wanted to see what you'd say.
(*They start moving pieces of furniture to accommodate the rug.*)
It's a nice bit of rug. (*Pause. He straightens up, considers it.*) Perhaps I've been rash. What do you think?

ANN: By all means, take it away again, if you want to.

DAVE: Very good for making love on, was that.

ANN: I never thought much of it.
(*Silence. They move the furniture back on to the rug.*)

DAVE: By the way, I meant to ask you, what was Patrick like in bed?

ANN: No worse than you.
(DAVE *is momentarily shaken, recovers quickly.*)

DAVE: No wonder you got rid of him, then.

190

(*The placing of the rug is now complete.*)
There. Everything to your satisfaction, madam?
(ANN *looks up at him, nods.*)

ANN: Except for one thing.

DAVE: I'm told you've left your job, as well.

ANN: Yes.

DAVE: About bloody time. Perhaps now you'll use your
qualifications for something more socially respectable.
Dubbing pornographic movies.
(ANN *sighs.*)
No, I'm serious. Lot of money in that. I know a bloke . . .

ANN: Look, why don't you take your chair, and get off back to
wherever you've come from.

DAVE: I don't think it would go in my room.

ANN: You're not still at the Savoy, are you?

DAVE: That's what my bank manager keeps saying.

ANN: I'm sure.

DAVE: Question of waiting till I can afford to pay the bill.
(*Silence. Their eyes meet.* DAVE *smiles.*)
Thirsty work.

ANN: What?

DAVE: Cuppa tea would be most welcome.

ANN: All right.

DAVE: Good gracious.
(ANN *exits to the kitchen.* DAVE *looks around the room, his face
serious. He moves over to the swivel-chair, is about to sit down,
then changes his mind and sits on the sofa.*)
Lonely?

ANN (*off*): What?

DAVE: Living on your own.

ANN (*off*): I like it.

DAVE: It has its advantages, doesn't it?

ANN (*off*): Yes.
(*Silence.* DAVE *checks his watch, considers a moment.*)

DAVE: You're not having Arthur back from the newsagent's,
then?
(ANN *comes in with two mugs of tea.*)

ANN: No, I thought about it, but I decided against it. (*She

191

hands DAVE *a mug, sits at the other end of the sofa.*)

DAVE: Thanks. (*He takes a sip.*) Oh, you remembered.

ANN: Four large sugars is hard to forget.

(DAVE *smiles.* ANN *sips at her tea. Silence.*)

DAVE: What made you get rid of Patrick?

ANN: Didn't work.

DAVE: Nice chap.

ANN (*suspiciously*): Yes.

DAVE: Full of over-educated bullshit, of course. Otherwise, I liked him. I never thought he was quite your speed.

ANN: Speed, of any kind, was not one of his strong points.

DAVE: His face, he looked like someone who'd just stepped into an empty lift-shaft. But then, so do most people nowadays, unless, like me, they actually enjoy dancing in the ruins.

ANN: And what are you up to at the moment?

DAVE: Nothing much. I went round to see Millicent again, having managed to conquer my invincible distaste for her name, but she seems to have taken up with an Australian poet, if you can imagine such a thing.

(*Silence.*)

What are you thinking of doing now?

ANN: I don't know, bit of a holiday, I should think, till the money runs out.

DAVE: Oh.

(*Silence.*)

ANN: Well, I'd say that just about wraps up the conversational possibilities, wouldn't you?

(*Silence.* DAVE *puts his cup down, looks across at* ANN.)

DAVE: Ann . . .

ANN: No.

DAVE: I wasn't going to say that.

ANN: What were you going to say?

DAVE: I was just going to say . . . what about another cup of tea?

ANN: That wasn't what you were going to say.

DAVE: No, you're quite right. I was just . . . wondering if you'd given any thought to that proposition I made the other evening.

ANN: What proposition?

DAVE: Proposal, I should say.

ANN: Oh.

DAVE: Well?

ANN: Yes, I have.

DAVE: I meant it, you know.

ANN: Yes.

DAVE: And . . . what have you decided?

ANN: I haven't changed my mind.

DAVE: Well, that's a relief.

ANN: Oh?

DAVE: Yes, your instinct was absolutely sound, it would have been a catastrophe.

ANN: I see.

DAVE: When I look around at the marriages of my friends, all I can see is . . . easy pickings.

ANN: That's an exaggeration.

DAVE: True. (*Pause.*) Still, as long as it lasts, the bad conscience of the female middle-class mafia, I guess there'll always be a niche for me.

ANN: Why do you hate women so much?

DAVE: I don't hate women.

ANN: Then why did you treat me so badly?

DAVE: Question is, why did you allow me to treat you so badly?

ANN: Do you mean you treated me badly because you hated me for letting you treat me badly?

DAVE: No, I mean I may have treated you badly because I thought you liked me to treat you badly.

ANN: I can't believe that.

DAVE: Patrick told me you'd never complained to him about me.

ANN: I didn't think it was any of his business. (*Pause.*) Were you pleased?

DAVE: No, I was rather annoyed. At first. Then I thought maybe I was on the wrong track all that time, since it doesn't seem to have had any effect. Still, I suppose we all make mistakes. As you no doubt said to Patrick.

ANN: Not an apology, is it?

DAVE: I expect it's the nearest you'll ever get to one.

ANN: Better make the most of it, then, hadn't I?

DAVE: It was what I was trying to tell you that evening I broke in.

ANN: Even then it was too late.

(Silence.)

DAVE: No reason . . . no reason we shouldn't see each other from time to time, is there?

ANN: What's the point?

DAVE: No point, I'd just like to know how you're getting on, that's all.

ANN: You're unusually mellow this afternoon.

(Silence.)

DAVE: What I was going to say, I mean what I actually was going to say when you stopped me just now, was, why don't we go to bed?

(Long silence.)

ANN: All right.

DAVE: What?

ANN: All right.

DAVE: Ah.

ANN: What's the matter?

DAVE: Nothing, you just, I don't know, caught me on the hop.

ANN: Well?

DAVE: Well . . . terrific.

(Silence. Neither of them moves.)

ANN: Then that'll be that.

DAVE: What do you mean?

ANN: What I say.

DAVE: Well, we'll see, shall we?

ANN: I'm telling you. *(Pause.)* I like things tidy.

(Silence.)

DAVE: O.K.

ANN: Right.

DAVE: It'll be; just a little treat.

ANN: Yes.

(Silence. They still haven't moved. DAVE *clears his throat.)*

DAVE: Well.

*(*ANN *gets up.)*

ANN: Bedroom?

(DAVE *smiles, recovered.*)

DAVE: Well, since I've gone to the trouble of humping this bloody great rug round . . .

ANN: If you insist.

DAVE: I do.

ANN: All right.

(DAVE *gets up.*)

DAVE: Funny.

ANN: What?

DAVE: I feel rather nervous. Reminds me of the night I lost my virginity, ha, what a card game that was.

(*He moves to* ANN, *takes her chin in his hand, looks at her for a moment, then turns away and crosses to the bedroom door, where he stops and turns back to* ANN.)

Get your clothes off, I won't be a minute.

(*He exits.* ANN *stands for a moment, then starts undressing. After a time,* DAVE *returns. He strides straight across to her and slaps her face hard.*)

I've changed my mind.

ANN: What?

DAVE: I've changed my mind. I don't know what it is you're up to, but I don't want anything to do with it.

ANN: What the hell are you talking about?

DAVE: Now, listen. I'm going back to the hotel now, and you can think about it this afternoon and this evening or however long it takes, and when you've made your mind up, you can ring me. Or not ring me, whatever you decide. Anyway, I'll be there. All right?

(*He moves over to the hall door.* ANN *watches him with hatred.*)

ANN: Is this what you planned, is it?

DAVE: I never make plans, I just live on my wits and try to cover all the exits. (*He smiles at her triumphantly.*) You just have to pick up the phone. (*He exits.*)

('*Will You Still Love Me Tomorrow?*' *sung by The Shirelles.*)

SCENE EIGHT

That evening. ANN, *alone, in a dressing-gown, sitting on the swivel-chair, facing front. She sits there for some time. Finally, she gets up, crosses to the television and switches it on. Instant picture. The actress should choose whichever channel seems most dramatically appropriate. She wanders back to the swivel-chair, turns it round and sits. She watches television for quite some time, invisible. Then she half-swivels round so that she is visible in profile. She is weeping. She weeps for a long time, finally sobbing uncontrollably. She stops suddenly, waits a moment, then gets up, crosses to the phone, picks up the receiver and dials.*

SCENE NINE

A week later. The room is now fully furnished, the empty bookshelf is full, there are more chairs, pictures on the wall. And so on. Evening.

ANN *and* DAVE *are sitting on the sofa, the remains of supper behind them on the dining-table, two glasses of brandy on the coffee-table in front of them.* ANN *is in her dressing-gown.* DAVE, *in shirtsleeves, is listening, through the headphones, to 'God' from the John Lennon L.P. 'Working-class Hero'. Fairly loud. Enjoying himself.*

After a time, from outside, the sound of breaking glass, followed immediately by frenzied barking. DAVE *looks across at* ANN, *takes the headphones off, gets up, crosses to the amplifier, puts the headphones down, takes the needle off the record, switches off and moves to the hall door. The barking continues throughout this.* DAVE *opens the hall door and steps into the hall.*

DAVE: Arthur. Arthur! Get down, boy.
    (*After a moment, he returns, shepherding* PATRICK. PATRICK'*s hand is bleeding. He stands just inside the door, hopelessly, white-faced.*)
    Arthur didn't do that, did he?
PATRICK: No, no, the, um, glass.
DAVE: Oh, I was going to say, if it was Arthur, we'd better get you down the doctor. Or him down the vet. You've given him a terrible turn.
PATRICK: I . . . (*He waves his bleeding hand at* ANN.) You see, not so neat, after all.
ANN: What are you talking about?
PATRICK: You . . .
ANN: Look, for God's sake, don't drip on the rug.
DAVE: Well, go on, get the poor bugger an Elastoplast or

197

something, don't just stand there.

(ANN *hesitates, then exits angrily to the bedroom.*)

PATRICK: I've just dropped by to have a word with you about stock-car racing.

DAVE: What?

PATRICK: Nothing.

DAVE: Are you quite all right?

(PATRICK *flaps his hand.*)

PATRICK: Apart from this.

DAVE: I think you'd better have a brandy.

(*He moves to the dining-recess, takes out a glass and pours a brandy.* ANN *returns from the bedroom with a bottle of T.C.P., cotton wool and a bandage. The two of them converge on* PATRICK *simultaneously. He takes the glass and submits his hand to* ANN *with some confusion.* DAVE *smiles, enjoying himself.*)

This is very trying, you know, we've only just had that pane replaced. The glazier will gossip. (*He swigs at his brandy.*) I must say, old bean, this shows a sad lack of imagination. Couldn't you have devised some other method? You could have bought a taxi and cruised around the area waiting to be hailed. Bit of originality, that's all we ask.

ANN: Stop it, Dave.

(*She concentrates on bandaging* PATRICK's *hand. He gazes at her miserably, speaks quietly to her.*)

PATRICK: I want to talk to you.

DAVE: We know that, Patrick, but I have to tell you this is not a convenient moment. We can't even offer you any supper, alas, I'm afraid we've scoffed the lot. So when you're all finished there, I'm sorry, but I'm going to have to ask you to slosh down your brandy and get off home to mother.

PATRICK: I have a flat of my own now.

DAVE: Then what you breaking in here for?

PATRICK: I've told you, I have to talk to Ann.

DAVE: And I've told you, this is not the right moment. Now, don't force me to get heavy with you. An Englishman's home is his castle, you know.

(ANN *finishes bandaging* PATRICK's *hand, breaks away from*

198

him.)

And, not to put too fine a point on it, if you're not out of
here in ten seconds, I'm going to call the police.

PATRICK: Look, I know it's difficult for you, but do you find it
quite impossible to be serious?

DAVE: You'd be surprised, mate. (*Pause.*) I'm waiting. (*Pause.*)
Right. (*He strides over to the telephone, lifts the receiver.*)

ANN: Don't.

(PATRICK *starts to move towards him, then freezes, panicked.*
DAVE *smiles at* ANN, *then dials* 999. *Moment of silence.*)

DAVE: Hello . . . oh, is there a choice? . . . I'll have to have a
think about it, I'll let you know. Thank you. (*He puts the
receiver down, smiling.*) Easy when you know how. (*Pause.*)
Next time I'll get them round here.

PATRICK: I don't understand this at all.

DAVE: There are no certainties in this world, Patrick. I have a
friend called Napoleon Bonaparte actually believes he's a
lunatic.

(*Silence.* PATRICK *bemused,* ANN *unhappy,* DAVE *confident.*)

ANN: I think perhaps you'd better go, Patrick.

(PATRICK *looks uncertainly from* ANN *to* DAVE.)

PATRICK: Are you going to get married?

DAVE: You're joking.

PATRICK: I just wondered.

DAVE: Look, in a couple of years' time or sooner or anyway
sometime we shall probably make a very unpleasant mess of
each other's lives and that'll be the end of it.

PATRICK: And is that . . . a reasonable basis?

DAVE: Of course it is, we just know in advance what catches
most people by surprise, that's all. (*Pause.*) Look, I tell you
what, I'm going away in a couple of weeks, why don't you
wait and have another bash then? If you get anywhere, of
course, you'll have to take into account the fact she's
probably only doing it to get back at me, but if you think
that's worthwhile, God bless you. Can't say fairer than
that, now can I? Alternatively, you could hang around until
the whole thing's over, although I shouldn't if I were you,
because I have to be honest with you, my money's on some

third party.

PATRICK: Ann.

DAVE: Let's leave it for now, shall we?

PATRICK: Did you read my letters?

DAVE: She wouldn't, I'm afraid, she's very stubborn. So I did. They were most affecting.

PATRICK: I'm talking to Ann.

DAVE: I know that, I can see that, but is she talking to you? That's the question we should be asking ourselves.

PATRICK: Look, will you . . .

DAVE: Patrick, I'm sorry about this, I really am, I like you, believe me, I've grown to be very fond of you. I mean, I won't deny this whole situation has a certain, you know, well, as an old mate of mine, Charlie Peters, always used to say, there is no more subtle pleasure than to see your best friend fall off the roof. But I do have a genuine affection and . . .

PATRICK: Fuck off!

DAVE: Patrick!

PATRICK: I'm talking to Ann!

DAVE: The floor is yours. (*He moves abruptly to the sofa, sits down, puts his feet up and watches them over the back of the sofa.*)

PATRICK: Ann.

DAVE: The rug is mine but the floor is yours.

(*He laughs, having been unable to resist this remark.* PATRICK, *however, takes no notice and moves closer to* ANN, *who has been growing increasingly tense, throughout these recent exchanges.*)

PATRICK: Is this what you want? That's all I want to ask you, love, I've done my best to be irrational this evening, but I can't understand, I can't bear to see this happening to you, so just tell me, it's all I want to know, is it, is this really what you want?

(*Silence. Suddenly,* ANN *bears down on* PATRICK, *furious.*)

ANN: Will you get the hell out of here, you stupid hopeless bastard, what the fuck do you think you're doing, can't you get it through your head, sod you, I want you out, understand that, can you, I want you out and I never want

200

to see you again!

(*Silence.* PATRICK *is stunned.*)

PATRICK: Well if you yes all right.

(*He turns, moves to the hall door, hesitates, turns back, shoots a helpless look round the room as if he thinks he's forgotten something, then exits into the hall.*

A second's silence, then ANN *suddenly runs after him into the hall, closing the door behind her.*

DAVE *sits up, startled by this.*

Long silence, during which DAVE's *face betrays a growing fear.*

The heavy sound of a door closing.

DAVE *starts to get up. He looks terrified.*

ANN *opens the door, stands in the doorway.*

DAVE *sits down again, looking at her.*

ANN *closes the door, advances into the room. She smiles at* DAVE.

DAVE *looks away from her, refusing to respond, stone-faced.*

As she draws level with him, still smiling, he looks up at her again, very cold.)